# WORLDS APART

# Praise for the book

"*Worlds Apart* is a powerful testament to resilience, connection, and to having the courage to dream beyond circumstance. Devi's journey – from studying under streetlights in Hyderabad to becoming a Network Engineer at Microsoft – is not just inspiring, it's transformational. This book is a celebration of what becomes possible when talent meets opportunity. We are proud to stand beside Devi and reaffirm our belief that when we lift others, we rise together."

—Puneet Chandok, President,
Microsoft India & South Asia

"*Worlds Apart* by Devi Boddu and Ed Cohen is a powerful story of courage, connection, and transformation. From a girl's dreams under a Hyderabad street lamp to a leader's journey of vulnerability, their intertwined paths show that lifting others lifts us all. This book redefines leadership as empathy and kindness, inspiring us to create ripples of change through small, authentic acts. A must-read for those who believe in the transformative power of human connection."

—Narayana Murthy, The visionary Founder of
Infosys and its Chairman Emeritus

"*Worlds Apart* is an extraordinary story of hope and connection. Devi's determination and Ed's honesty come together in a way that makes you believe in the ripple effect of kindness. It's a reminder that small acts can spark life-changing journeys."

—Gul Panag, Actor, Entrepreneur, and Social Activist

"I do believe this story will resonate with every other middle-class family in India who have clawed their way out of poverty through the power of education and self-reliance. And similarly with every wealthy family who made it from nothing as well. Starting with determination, finding a mentor, that one person who saw them for what they were capable of, and who helped them on. Along with the herculean effort and emotional resilience to keep doing all it takes, through ups and downs without self-destruction or doubt, to make it through. And finally to in turn carry the encouragement forward to help another out of poverty and misery. This is the story of humanity, of India and every family who aspires for a better life."

—Amala Akkineni, Actor, Social Activist, and
Director of Annapurna College of Film and Media

"*Worlds Apart* is a profoundly moving story that touches at the heart of empathy, the impact of learning and unlearning, and a deep sense of altruism. *Worlds Apart* shows us the power of connections that truly transcends both geographic and cultural barriers, and how hope triumphs over adversity and overcoming circumstance. Through the remarkable journeys of Devi Boddu and Ed Cohen, we witness how compassion, mentorship, and courage can transform lives—and in doing so, transform the way we lead."

—Dr. Mukesh Aghi, President and CEO,
U.S.-India Strategic Partnership Forum (USISPF)

"Ed's story touched me in an equally profound way. He did not enter Devi's life as a saviour; he came carrying his own scars and silences. What makes his journey remarkable is that he allowed her resilience to change him. Through Devi, he discovered that real strength lies in honesty, vulnerability, and in standing beside someone rather than above them. *Worlds Apart* reminds us that opportunity must be created and protected, and that no dream is ever too small."

—Sita Pallacholla, CEO, WE Hub, Founder,
The Angel Hub, Community Builder, Entrepreneur

"*Worlds Apart* reminds us how deeply connected we truly are. A single act of kindness not only transformed a future but also unlocked years of silence and hidden pain."

—Dinesh Neelakandan, Film Maker

"I have had the privilege of knowing Devi and Ed personally, and of witnessing the extraordinary relationship at the heart of *Worlds Apart*. This deeply moving yet uplifting true story transcends borders, cultures, and generations. It is a powerful journey of resilience, compassion, and transformation. This book is not just about two lives; it's about what becomes possible when we choose to notice and uplift one another. A timely, hopeful, and necessary read for anyone who believes in the power of human connection to change the world."

—Pragnya Seth, Executive Coach, Consultant

"I have had the opportunity of walking beside Ed Cohen for nearly twenty years as my Manager, Mentee, and someone I now call family. From the moment Ed and his wife, Pris came into my life, they gave me more than just guidance. Reading *Worlds Apart* felt very personal because I have lived through the kind of change this book talks about. Devi's journey is a reminder of the strength so many carry --often in silence. Ed's compassion, helping nature, and authentic leadership shine through. And, Devi's path shows what is possible when determination meets opportunity. This is not just the story of two people, it's proof of what can happen when we lead with care, trust, and genuine human connection. It's a story that will touch your heart and stay with you."

—Sunita Lanka, Global Operations Leader,
SprintRay India

"What makes this book stand out is its seamless blend of personal narrative and universal insight. Is it a self-help book, a leadership guide, or a masterclass in emotional intelligence and vulnerability? In truth, it is all three. This isn't just a book to read—it's one to experience, apply, and grow from. Having worked closely with Ed and witnessed his heart-led leadership,

I can say *Worlds Apart* reflects the compassionate, grounded leadership he lives every day. For anyone seeking meaning, growth, or a way to make a positive impact, *Worlds Apart* is essential reading."

—S. Abhirama Krishna, Director General,
Badruka Group of Institutions, Hyderabad, India

# WORLDS APART

## A True Story of Courage, Connection, and Change

DEVI BODDU    ED COHEN

Om Books International

First published in 2026 by

**Om Books International**

**Corporate & Editorial Office**
A-12, Sector 64, Noida 201 301
Uttar Pradesh, India
Phone: +91 120 477 4100
Email: editorial@ombooks.com
Website: www.ombooksinternational.com

**Sales Office**
107, Ansari Road, Darya Ganj,
New Delhi 110 002, India
Phone: +91 11 4000 9000
Email: sales@ombooks.com
Website: www.ombooks.com




ISBN: 978-93-6395-245-4

Printed in India

10 9 8 7 6 5 4 3 2 1

*For anyone who has ever been told to stay quiet, to stop dreaming, or to accept a life that was never truly theirs—this book is for you.*

*And to every girl who still fights for her right to learn, to speak, and to choose her own future—may you know how powerful you are.*

*You alone have the right to your dreams. No one can stop you.*

*You can write your own destiny—just believe in yourself once.*

"Let us sacrifice our today so that our children can have a better tomorrow."

—Dr A.P.J. Abdul Kalam

# Contents

# Foreword

## Arvind Krishna

## Who is a guru?

In India, a guru is someone who lights the path when you cannot see the way. Someone who believes in your potential long before you do.

For me, that someone is Ed Cohen.

## Picture this:

A young graduate from the University of Southern California (USC) walks into an interview with a senior vice president. Later, he ends the conversation with a casual, "Thanks, dude."

Most would assume that's the end of the story—a missed opportunity, a lesson in corporate etiquette.

But Ed saw something else.

He saw a spark, a spirit. And a few days later, I got the call: I was in!

At the time, I didn't realise how rare that was. I didn't understand that Ed wasn't merely offering me a job—he was opening a door into a way of living and leading that would shape my entire future.

I began my career at the Satyam School of Leadership, the youngest on the team. Years later, when I became an actor, an international athlete, and a voice for veganism and sustainability, people often asked me how I managed to lead a life across such different worlds. The truth is—it started there. It started with Ed.

He taught me that leadership isn't about being the loudest in the room—it's about being the clearest. Not the most powerful, but the most honest. And sometimes, the most vulnerable.

One memory I'll always carry with me:

In those early days, I wore an ear stud to work. Not exactly traditional corporate attire—especially not in the world of leadership development. But Ed didn't just tolerate it. He celebrated it.

One day, he showed up wearing an ear stud himself. Not to match me, but to send a message.

Soon, half the team followed.

It wasn't about fashion. It was about belonging.

Ed's leadership wasn't rooted in hierarchy. It was rooted in humanity. He made sure everyone had a place at the table, just as they were.

He also saw potential in me that I hadn't yet recognised. After reading an email I'd written, he made me the editor of our leadership journal—even though I was the least experienced on the team. That trust gave me the chance to refine my writing, lead editorial meetings with senior colleagues, and find my voice.

Ed also noticed my passion for public speaking and facilitation. He invested in my development and gave me the chance to run sessions for senior teams—a rare honour for someone my age. That was Ed's way: recognising and nurturing potential, not just measuring performance.

Reading *Worlds Apart* brought it all back.

In these pages, you'll meet Ed and Devi—two people from entirely different worlds. Different countries, different generations, different struggles. And yet, a simple act of kindness—a teenage girl saying "Hey" to another girl sitting alone—changed everything.

When I first met Devi as a young girl, I could tell she was full of light and hope. I remember wishing she'd find the opportunities to realise her potential—to use education to grow into the best version of herself and make a positive impact. Because of the close bond we shared at the Satyam School of Leadership, many of us, myself included, stayed connected to her journey. Through Ed, we received updates, met her on occasions, and watched her blossom into a confident, capable professional. I couldn't be prouder of how far she's come and how much she's overcome.

Her story is a testament to resilience, mentorship, and what becomes possible when someone believes in you—and you begin to believe in yourself.

It reminded me of something else Ed taught me:

Leadership begins with noticing.

Noticing who's sitting alone.

Noticing who feels invisible.

Noticing when someone needs a hand—or simply someone who believes in them.

Ed grew up with his own struggles—a childhood marked by fear and silence. Devi grew up fighting for a future she was told she couldn't have. But both chose courage over resignation. Vulnerability over protection. Connection over separation.

Reading this book, I saw echoes of my own journey.

I was bullied as a child. For a long time, I carried those wounds silently. Healing didn't mean forgetting—it meant facing those scars without shame, and choosing to lead anyway.

Choosing to believe in others anyway.

That's what *Worlds Apart* is really about.

It's not about saviours or heroes. It's about fellow travellers. It's about showing up, not ahead of someone—but beside them.

Today, as a father, I see these lessons more clearly than ever.

To truly lead—whether a team, a family, or even yourself—you must meet people where they are. You must help heal, not just instruct. And often, the bravest thing you can do is let people see your whole, imperfect self.

Education was the bridge that changed Devi's life. It was also Ed's escape from fear. And it was mine.

Now imagine a world where every child has access to that bridge.

A world where every child is free to dream, to heal, to lead.

That's the world we must work towards. Because education is not only about literacy. It's about unlocking human potential, uplifting communities, and building a future free from poverty.

If you allow it, *Worlds Apart* will shift the way you think about leadership, success, and even love.

It's not a typical leadership book. It's not a typical journey.

It's a mirror—one that shows us who we are, and who we can become, if we dare to lead with heart.

So as you turn these pages, I invite you to do what Ed taught me:

Notice.

Notice the strength in vulnerability.

Notice the courage in connection.

Notice the possibilities—in yourself, and in others.

And maybe, just maybe, you'll light the path for someone else too.

—**Arvind Krishna** is an award-winning actor, international athlete, and passionate advocate for sustainability, veganism, and compassion. Best known for his acclaimed performances in *It's My Love Story* and *Rushi,* and his recent lead role in *A Masterpiece,* Arvind inspires across film, sport, and global leadership arenas with his relentless commitment to creativity, courage, and positive change.

# Prologue
# When Two Worlds Collide

**How far apart can two lives begin—and still come together in a story where each of us sees a piece of ourselves?**

Before we begin, I ask only this: Read with your heart as much as your mind. Let go of what you think you already know—about poverty and privilege, about giving and receiving, about who lifts whom, and how. Come not with judgment, but with curiosity.

Because this is not only my story. It is not only hers, either. And in some way, it may turn out to be yours too.

Some lives move in parallel—separated by geography, shaped by different customs, or confined by invisible boundaries we seldom question. But now and then, life intervenes. It offers a nudge, a crossing of paths, a single moment—a knock at the door, a brief conversation, or a small decision—that changes everything.

I was born in America—a country widely seen as a land of opportunity. It was the 1960s, a time of great transformation. The world watched as people marched for civil rights, as rockets rose toward the moon, and as voices called out for change. Yet inside our home, those sweeping dreams did not find a place to settle. From the outside, we appeared to be a typical middle-class family. But behind the facade was a truth that few saw. I had only one pair of shoes, and I wore them with care. The walls around me were strong, but they did not protect me from what lay within. I learned early how to be invisible, how to listen without speaking, how to sense danger before it arrived. The house looked safe. But my life inside it was not.

She was born decades later, in 1995, in a small village in South India—a place where tradition often spoke louder than ambition, especially for girls. In her world, daughters were expected to be modest, obedient, and to tuck their dreams into corners where they wouldn't be noticed. Education was respected, of course, but rarely pursued with the same energy or resources given to boys. Yet, even in that setting, she carried within her a determination—a belief that her life could grow beyond what was written for her. She went to school, not with advantage, but with intent. No private tutors. No quiet rooms. Just books balanced on hope.

Later, her family moved to Hyderabad—then a city on the cusp of transformation. The tech industry was beginning to rise, and opportunity pulsed through the air. Glass buildings stood beside ancient ones. Change was visible, yet uneven. In the narrow lanes behind her mother's employer's house, she would sit outside in the driveway, under a single flickering bulb, and study while the city slept. Her schoolbag often became her pillow. Her determination, her only constant.

We were never meant to meet. There was no reason our lives should have crossed—an American executive and a young Indian girl, each carrying a past the other couldn't begin to imagine.

But in 2006, in a calm lane in Hyderabad, things shifted. Not with any ceremony. Just a moment between two girls—my daughter, MacKenzie, then 15, and Devi Boddu, who was 12.

MacKenzie was lonely. We had just moved across the world, and everything felt unfamiliar. Devi lived with her family in a single room behind her mother's employer's house. She studied in the driveway each night because it was the only quiet space she had.

MacKenzie reached out, simply and sincerely, and invited her in. That gesture—the kindness of a teenager—opened a door in more ways than one.

At first, it seemed simple. A girl with bright eyes and big dreams. A family willing to open its heart. I thought we were helping her. That we were giving her a better chance.

But gradually, the story began to turn. Because what she brought into our lives wasn't just gratitude or perseverance. She brought warmth. She brought clarity. She brought reminders of wounds I had buried so deeply, I had forgotten they were still there.

I had spent most of my adult life behind a mask—the polished mask of leadership, of control, of capability. I was the one with answers, the one others came to for direction. But behind all of that were old scars. Formed in silence. Covered by roles and responsibilities.

I had convinced myself that I had moved on. But standing before me was a girl who refused to bend. Even when the odds were stacked against her. Even when life kept saying no.

She didn't just need support. She reflected back to me something I had long forgotten: That strength is not in pretending to be fine. It is in showing up anyway.

Years later, I shared a small part of this story online. I wrote a short post about Devi—about her fight for education, and about the way our lives had become intertwined.

I didn't expect much.

But the post spread like wild jasmine in summer. It crossed oceans, platforms, and borders. Within weeks, more than eight million people had read it. And with it came the unexpected: Messages from strangers. Teachers. Students. Parents. Leaders. People who saw themselves in her journey. People who saw themselves in mine.

What began with an invitation had become a conversation—about belief, about kindness, and about what it truly means to lift someone. Not from above, but beside.

**Here's what I wrote in that 2025 LinkedIn post:**

This year marked 20 years since we moved to India—a journey that transformed our lives in many ways. One of the most memorable lessons came from a 12-year-old girl named Devi Boddu, whose story continues to inspire.

Devi lived with her family in a single room behind her mother's employer's house. She studied in the driveway to avoid distractions and often slept there just to wake up early and make the most of her time.

When my family welcomed her into our home, we didn't realize the ripple effect it would create. Shared meals, encouragement, and treating her as an equal gave her confidence to dream bigger.

Today, Devi is a Networking Engineer at Microsoft—a testament to her resilience and the power of opportunity.

Her story taught me: – Believing in someone's potential unlocks possibilities they may not yet see.

– Small acts of kindness create lasting change.

– When we lift others, we rise with them.

The most powerful lesson was about vulnerability: by opening our hearts, we created space for both of us to grow.

What I had not shared was that Devi's struggle was also mine.

How a determined girl in India helped a man from the other side of the world confront his own past.

How one act of kindness changed her future—and mine as well.

Little did we know, the real collision of our worlds would not happen in a single moment—it would unfold through a shared struggle, through fears that mirrored each other across continents.

This story may begin with two people, once worlds apart. But by the end, it may just belong to you too.

Two people. Two continents. Two lives marked by hardship, yet joined by a single act of kindness.

This is a story rooted in both our lives. And yet, beyond the one we wrote, there may be another waiting to be told. Perhaps it is yours.

Because what you choose to carry forward from this story—that is where the real journey begins.

Now that the door has opened, I cannot pretend I did not hear the knock. Not anymore. And maybe now, you have heard it too.

This book is not here to give you answers. It is an invitation. To look again—at yourself, at those around you, and at the invisible lines we have learned to draw between "us" and "them."

It is about what happens when we choose to truly see one another. When we pause long enough to say: I may not know your full story, but I will not look away.

So read slowly. Breathe between the lines. And if something stirs—stay with it.

Because sometimes, the stories that change us the most do not shout. They whisper.

And they begin with a gentle knock at the door.

# Part 1

# Two Worlds, One Journey

"You may never know what results come of your actions. But if you do nothing, there will be no result."

—Mahatma Gandhi

# Chapter 1

# Devi's Childhood of Dreams

I was born into a world where dreams were not luxuries—they were acts of defiance. Nandyal, a small town nestled between the Nallamala and Erramala hill ranges in south India, was the only world I had ever known. Here, life was both simple and unyielding, shaped by the rhythm of the land and the silent endurance of its people. Sometimes, I would wake up before dawn and listen to the roosters crowing, feeling a peace in my heart because I knew exactly what the day would bring. A part of me also wondered if I would ever see beyond these fields and dusty roads.

## My Name is Devi

My full name is Chamundeshwari Devi, but it became just Devi—because of me.

As a little girl, I didn't yet understand the weight names could carry. I only knew that I wanted mine to be simpler. So I began to call myself Devi. Not out of rebellion, but out of a desire to shape my identity on my terms. I wanted to stand out in a place where tradition often writes your story before you can hold a pen.

I didn't yet understand the hardship my mother endured, the sacrifices etched into the lines of her palm. The rough and uneven roads wound their way through fields of rice, cotton, and groundnuts—the lifeblood of our community. Agriculture wasn't just an occupation; it was the fine balance between survival and scarcity.

Uncertainty loomed over our lives—like the monsoon that either nourished us or destroyed everything .

At dawn, the fields stirred with life as men toiled under the burden of their labour, their hands gnarled with calluses, their skin tanned by the relentless sun. After irrigation, the air carried the scent of damp earth, mingling with the acrid tang of sweat and the smoke from distant cooking fires.

Almost every morning, Amma would wake up before the first whisper of dawn and bring a small steel tumbler filled with steaming milk tea for me. "Devi," she would say gently, "finish this quickly." I would sip the tea, still half-asleep, feeling its warmth spread through my body. Then, stepping outside, I would see the first rays of sunlight breaking through the sky, turning everything into the hues of soft pink-orange.

Sometimes, as I held the tumbler, I would ask, "Why do we wake up so early, Amma?" She would smile and reply, "Because the day doesn't wait for us. We must go and catch it." Her words made me feel as if each morning was an adventure I could not afford to miss.

For many women in our village, the day began before the sun even showed its face. My Amma—Mahalakshmi—was no different. She never worked outside home until we moved to Hyderabad. She was married very young and spent her life with my father. Though she hadn't been taught in school, she held a strength that shaped our home.

She was always doing—cooking, cleaning, caring. My father was a tailor, and together, they created a life filled with warmth and simplicity. They were happy and, whatever they had, they made it enough.

The market was a world of its own, alive with colour and sound—the clatter of metal coins, exchanging hands, the sharp scent of turmeric and dried chillies hanging thick in the air, and the rhythmic bargaining between buyer and seller felt like a song.

Sometimes, on days when we didn't go to school, my sister Jyothi and I would accompany Amma to the market. The noise and bright colours dazzled me. She would instruct us quietly, "Stand here. Watch our baskets," while she spoke to the buyers. I loved seeing her negotiate with such confidence, though she was soft-spoken at home. By the time we finished, my feet would be dusty, and my heart felt light because I was helping Amma in my own small way.

Our home, like most of them in the village, was simple—a small house with cracked mud walls. The mud floor was cool in winter but suffocating in the peak of summer. Most households in Nandyal didn't have running water; that remained a distant dream. Our lives were shaped by patience, not convenience. Water was a daily mission, and it shaped our routines, especially for women and children.

Every morning, Amma or Jyothi would carry heavy metal pots and walk to the communal tap. Water was required for daily needs like washing clothes, bathing, or doing dishes, it was released through a tap installed on every street.

These taps were functional only during specific hours— usually early in the morning and occasionally in the late afternoon. We would wait for our turn in a long queue with other women, all of us hoping the water supply wouldn't stop before our pots were filled. On hot days or when the supply was low, the wait could stretch for more than an hour. Sometimes we had to go again just to fetch enough water for the family.

It wasn't just about water—it was about endurance, patience, and community. It was also about the unseen labour that women and children put in each day just to have access to the most basic needs.

Drinking water came from the village well. That well was more than just a source of water—it was where the stories were exchanged, worries were whispered, and laughter mingled with the splash of filled pots. Some days, if we were lucky, there was no queue. Other days, especially in summer, the wait could stretch for hours.

The women stood in queue, shifting the heavy brass pots from one arm to the other, discussing the day's work, the harvest, and the latest happenings in the village.

"Yesterday, the landlord's daughter returned from Hyderabad," one woman said, adjusting the end of the sari over her shoulder.

"Ah, city life must be so easy. Imagine—turning a knob of the tap and water comes straight into your house," another would sigh, shaking her head.

"We have no such luck," Amma would reply, gripping her pot tightly. "Until then, we carry on."

Fetching water was less a chore and more a way of life. It wasn't costly to use the well, but that didn't mean it was easy. In summer, when the water level dropped, the strongest women would have to pull it up using thick ropes tied to the pots, straining with all their strength. If the well dried up completely, we had to walk even farther towards another well or to a public hand pump.

For many, fetching water wasn't just hard—it was dangerous.

One morning, as we waited in queue, an older woman shook her head and muttered, "This well has taken more than it has given."

I turned to her, curious. "What do you mean, Amma *garu?*"

She exhaled sharply. "My elder sister ... when she was only thirteen, she was pulling water from this well. She lost her balance and fell in. By the time anyone pulled her out, it was too late."

The other women sighed and nodded knowingly. This wasn't the first story of its kind. The well had no barriers, no protection, just crumbling stone around its edges. The danger was real: in the dark, or with tired, slippery hands, anyone could lose their grip.

I choked back my fear, suddenly more aware of the deep, gaping pothole just a few feet away. I tightened my grip on my pot.

"Devi, hold this properly!" Amma scolded me once when I nearly tipped over the pot.

"But, Amma, my arms are aching," I whined, struggling under the weight.

She clicked her tongue in disapproval and adjusted the pot on my hip. "You will get used to it. See, Jyothi is carrying without complaining."

I glanced at my sister, who balanced her pot like it weighed nothing. She smirked at me. "You have weak hands," she teased.

I scowled but said nothing. That night, I lay awake thinking about the woman's story about the thirteen-year-old girl who never returned home.

The next morning, when it was my turn to fetch water from the well, I gripped the rope a little more firmly.

Washing clothes was another water-dependent task. Since we didn't have enough at home, we carried the clothes to the river or to a nearby water tank. There, women sat in rows, scrubbing fabric against stones, their hands rough from the harsh soap. The rhythmic beating of wet clothes intertwined with chatter and bursts of laughter.

"Amma, why do we wash clothes here?" I asked one day, watching her wring out a sari.

"Because at home, we can't waste water," she said, shaking off the excess and laying the fabric on a rock to dry.

Bathing was no less of a struggle. At home, we used tiny buckets, scooping water over ourselves with a metal mug. During the hottest months, some people bathed at the river, but Amma never let us go there.

"It's not safe for girls," she would say firmly. "Men go there, and the water level is deep."

Instead, she heated water over the fire when she could, and we would bathe quickly, using just enough to rinse away the dust of the day. There was no luxury of long baths or privacy— just a quick splash before the next task.

Every drop was precious—we carried, saved, and never wasted. I often wondered what it would be like to turn a knob of a tap and see water flow freely, like people said it happened in big cities.

"Akka," I asked Jyothi one night as we lay on our mats, "do you think one day we will have taps in our house?"

She turned on her side, thinking. "Maybe." she said. "But until then, we carry on."

I closed my eyes, dreaming of a world where we would not have to.

Sometimes I wished we had just one photo of our family to hang on the wall. Whenever I mentioned it, Amma would say, "We cannot eat a photograph. Better we spend that money on food." I understood her reasoning, but a small part of me still longed for a framed memory of us together.

## Crowded Nights, Quiet Thoughts

At night, the room felt even smaller as we squeezed together to sleep. There was no privacy, no space beyond the confines of necessity.

At times during the night, when sleep eluded me, I would whisper to Jyothi, "Akka, do you think there is a world outside Nandyal with bright lights and tall buildings?" She would smile drowsily and say, "Maybe, Devi. But we have our own bright lights as stars here." She would point to the cracks in the roof, where tiny slivers of the night sky peeked through. I would stare at those stars, my mind drifting—half-wishing I could follow them beyond our village, a little afraid of what lies beyond.

## My Town, Nandyal

Despite its hardships, Nandyal had its own beauty. It was a place rich in history and spirituality, surrounded by the nine sacred temples known as the Nava Nandi. Pilgrims often travelled here, their voices carrying prayers into the wind, blending with the distant chime of temple bells. The towering stone idols, weathered by time, stood as silent witnesses to the countless generations that had passed through this land.

Beyond its spiritual significance, Nandyal was transforming. The town was growing, and industries like rice mills, oil mills, and cotton factories had taken root. Some families found work in these businesses, earning slightly more than what the land could offer. The most ambitious among us dreamed of moving to places like Hyderabad, where the future seemed brighter, where a child's education could mean more than just learning how to survive.

Yet, for most of us, life remained the same. The men in our village rarely spoke about their dreams—only about crops and rainfall, debts and hands that ached from ploughing. The women didn't speak of ambitions beyond their families; they simply worked, their bodies weathered by years of household chores, and carrying burdens far heavier than their thin frames should have endured.

## Amma's Strength

Amma, though only in her twenties, looked older. The years of relentless work had carved lines into her face, and her once-smooth hands had turned rough and cracked. Yet, there was something steady in her eyes and it was unshakable.

Every day was similar. "Devi, wake up," she would call softly, her voice firm yet gentle, waking me from sleep. "The day will not wait for us."

I would sit groggily, holding the thin blanket I shared with Jyothi. The air inside our small house was thick with the lingering warmth of bodies pressed together through the night. Outside, the first sounds of the village waking up drifted in—the distant creak of wooden carts being pulled onto the road, the murmurs of women gathering water from the communal well, the occasional cry of a baby roused by the morning bustle.

Amma's presence was my anchor. No matter how tired she was, she carried herself with resolve, moving through life with a determination I could not yet fully understand. She never complained, never relented to rest, as if she had long since learnt to ignore exhaustion.

Yet, when I looked at her, I sometimes wondered what she saw when she looked at me. Did she see a child, or did she see a girl who, too, would one day carry her own burdens? Did she ever dream of a life beyond this endless cycle of work? I hoped so.

She never spoke of such things, but the truth often lingered in the silence between her words. Whenever I looked into her eyes, she would give me a little, warm smile and say, "I have you. What else do I need?"

She meant it. I knew she did. Yet, at night, when she thought I was asleep, I would sometimes hear her let out a sigh—one that seemed to carry the weight of a thousand unspoken dreams.

If Amma had been given the chance to rest—to dream beyond survival—would she have taken it? Or had she long ago made peace with her reality, choosing instead to pour everything she had into making sure that our future would be different?

I would close my eyes and hope that one day, I could give her the comfort she deserved.

## "Not for Girls..."

In Nandyal, education for girls wasn't considered a priority. Many families believed that schooling was a luxury, even though it did not offer immediate returns. Conventional practices placed a greater emphasis on domestic responsibilities, and for many, a girl's education was merely a way to keep her occupied until marriage. While boys were encouraged to study and build careers, girls were expected to focus on household chores, reinforcing the belief that a woman's future depended more on her ability to run a home than on her academic achievements.

Despite this, some progress had been made. Government initiatives provided financial support to encourage female education, and the rate of enrolment in primary schools had improved significantly. Yet, the challenges were still there. Most of the girls in Andhra attended primary school, but drop out rates increased at the secondary and higher secondary levels. Financial hardships, early marriages, and the perception that higher education was unnecessary for girls prompted families to withdraw them from school.

Amma never stopped Jyothi or me from going to school, though she did not fully understand its value initially. For her, survival depended on hard work, not books. Education had not been much of an option in her life, and she had learnt to navigate the world through sheer resilience. To her, school was just another part of our routine—keeping us busy while she worked.

I perceived it differently. School wasn't just a place to pass the time; it was an escape, a window into a much larger world. The lessons, taught entirely in Telugu, often felt like puzzles I struggled to piece together. Every new word I learnt felt like a tiny key unlocking a door to a future beyond what I knew.

For girls like me, education was more than just a classroom experience. It was an act of defiance, a challenge to a world that often said, "Not for girls."

Still, doubt often crept in. Sometimes, in class, I would hear the other children chattering confidently while I stumbled over my words, feeling like I was the only one who did not understand. My heart would race, and I would worry that maybe I wasn't smart enough. Jyothi would try to reassure me at home, saying, "Devi, you're the brightest among us!" Her kind words could not always drown out the voice in my head telling me I'd never catch up.

One day, after weeks of struggling with a math problem, I finally realised that I couldn't do it on my own anymore. With nervousness, I approached my teacher after the class, clutching the notebook like it was a lifeline.

"Madam," I began, my voice barely a whisper, "can you help me? I'm not … I'm not able to understand this."

She looked at me with warmth in her eyes and smiled. "Of course, Devi," she said, her voice soft yet steady. "Let's work on this together."

For the next hour, she patiently guided me through the steps over and over, using chalk, hand movements, and even small objects from the classroom to make me see the problem in a new way. Gradually, the numbers began to make sense. When I finally solved the problem on my own, my heart swelled with pride.

"See?" she said, her eyes sparkling. "I told you, you could do it."

Her faith in me became a turning point. I wasn't just solving maths problems—I was overcoming a part of myself that always told me I wasn't enough. From that moment, a small spark ignited within me. Maybe I could do more than just exist in Nandyal. Maybe there was a greater world waiting for me.

My father was a tailor. He spent long hours bent over fabric, his fingers moving with precision as he stitched clothes for people in the village. He didn't talk much, but he noticed everything. His silence was steady, like the hum of his sewing machine—constant, unassuming, always in the background.

That evening, I excitedly showed Amma my notebook, pointing out the recently solved sums. She stroked my hair gently with affection and said, "I knew you'd figure it out, Devi. You always do." Her eyes sparkled with pride, the kind that made me want to try even harder.

I turned to show Nana. Amma stood behind me, smiling. He looked quietly at the page, then at me. He didn't say much—but he nodded. That was enough. I cherished his acknowledgement like a medal.

## Leaving Nandyal

A few days later, everything changed.

"We are leaving Nandyal," Amma said in Telugu, our mother tongue. Her voice was soft but resolute. "I have got a job in Hyderabad."

Hyderabad—a name too big for my young mind to understand—hung silently in the air. I had heard of it—*peddha pattinam*, the big city—crowded with people, dazzling with lights, and populated with strangers. I had never imagined living there.

I turned to Jyothi. She sat silently, but her eyes also betrayed the swirl of emotions I felt—fear, hope, confusion.

"What job, Amma?" she asked.

"I will work for a lady, Raji Madam. Cleaning, cooking … it's a good job. We'll have a place to stay."

I hesitated. "Will Nana come with us?"

Amma's face stayed still. "No. He will remain here. He has to work."

A feeling of void developed inside me. Nana had always come for a while and then went for his  tailoring work, but this time, it felt final. His absence wouldn't be temporary anymore—it would be permanent.

Still, Amma didn't take us immediately. She left first, leaving us alone, to begin the job and settle in. Jyothi and I stayed behind in Boyalakuntla, with Nana and our grandmother. Though Nana was gentle, he spoke little. Amma was the center of our world, and without her, everything felt off balance.

Some days, I would wander down the road without any direction, hoping somehow my footsteps would lead me to her. When they didn't, I cried. Jyothi, just a little older, became my refuge. "Devi," she'd whisper. "Amma will come back for us."

And she did.

After one long year, Raji Madam gave Amma permission to bring her children. That's when the course of our lives truly shifted. Amma wasn't just working for our daily needs anymore—she was working for our future.

During that year, Jyothi and I studied at the government school in the village. The classrooms were bare, the benches hard, but the teachers were kind. Each night, I would look up at the sky and wonder if Amma could see the same moon from Hyderabad.

That night, before we were to leave, Jyothi and I lay awake on our thin mats. The oil lamp flickered dimly, throwing restless shadows on the mud walls.

I could hear her breathing—uneven, shallow. She was awake, holding back tears.

"Devi, *nidra raadha?*" she whispered.

"Yes, Akka," I murmured. "You can't sleep either?"

She turned toward me. "I'm scared," she said softly. "What if we don't like Hyderabad? What if they laugh at us for speaking like villagers?"

Her words echoed the thoughts I hadn't spoken aloud, twisting my stomach into a knot.

"I keep wondering about that too. It's such a big place— *enta peddadhi*—where will we belong?" I hesitated. "And Nana… he'll be here alone. Maybe he doesn't want us. Or maybe we just don't understand him."

Jyothi sighed. "Amma said he has his reasons. But it still hurts." She paused. "Will I finish school there? Or will Amma want me to work too?"

I didn't know. "Maybe there's a school nearby?" I offered, though my voice lacked conviction.

She nodded faintly, tension tightened the muscles in her face. "You're the smart one, Devi. Don't lose what you've learned. I'm proud of you."

I felt a pang of sadness and a surge of warmth all at once in my heart.

"But Akka," I whispered, "I don't want to leave this place. I'm scared Amma will work very hard again."

Moonlight crept through the cracks in the roof, tracing silver lines across the room. Our small bundle of belongings huddled in the corner—silent witnesses to our goodbye.

Jyothi reached for my hand and gave it a gentle squeeze.

"We have each other," she said, trying to sound brave. "That's something, right?"

I forced my tears away. "Yes, Akka. It's something."

Despite the swirl of strangers, a warmth settled in my chest. No matter how vast or unfamiliar Hyderabad might be, if we had each other, maybe—just maybe—we would find our way.

As a child, I couldn't yet grasp the weight Amma bore, the sacrifices tucked into her silence. I only knew that life wasn't what we shaped—it was what we endured. I was beginning to understand that dreams come with a cost—and that some people are never even given the chance to dream at all.

# Chapter 2

# Ed's House of Shadows

For as long as I can remember, I have struggled to make sense of the world around me. What does a child truly understand about injustice? About the weight of limitations that are placed even before dreams can take shape? Years before Devi carried the burden of expectations in Nandyal, I was already caught in my own silent war—a battle that shaped the person I was destined to become.

The path of survival is seldom straight. Sometimes, it begins in a town where tradition dictates a child's future before birth. At other times, it unfolds behind closed doors, in a home that should offer safety but instead becomes a place of fear. My story began in 1959—not in India, but in Chicago—in a small, shared house divided into two modest units. One of them was ours.

From the outside, it looked like any other home. But inside, it was cold and stifling—a space where hope was choked off before it could breathe. The walls did more than separate rooms; they swallowed our cries, silenced our dreams, and held us in a kind of relentless stillness. Even the silence had weight, a heaviness that lingered in the air. Fear clung to every corner—persistent and stable.

My father's temper flared up without warning—like an out-of-season monsoon, fierce and uninvited. It had little to do with the lack of discipline, and everything to do with the pain he had inherited—a poison seeping through generations. The echo of his fury resided in the room long after he was gone. I sometimes still feel the weight pressing on my chest—the heaviness that shaped the boy I was, and the mask I wore for many years.

## Dinner Time: A Moment of Dread

By the time I was nine, we had moved to Miami—a city of striking contrasts in the late 1960s. To the outsiders it appeared like a dream. Palm trees along every road, the sea breeze carried the aroma of Cuban coffee, and pastel-coloured buildings ablaze in the golden light of the setting sun. Tourists came in search of beaches, music, and the illusion of escape.

But beneath that postcard beauty, Miami was a city in flux—growing rapidlyly, yes, but also grappled with rising crime, social unrest, and widening inequality. The glamour was real, but so was the danger.

Of course, that wasn't the Miami we knew.

We lived far from the glossy waterfront homes and lively tourist spots—in a quieter part of town where families worked hard just to make ends meet. The locality was modest and mostly peaceful, but it had its own struggles. The pavement was cracked, the heat lingered even after sunset, and a kind of uneasy quietness filled the air. People were friendly to each other, and it seemed like everyone knew each other's business.

Life moved at its own pace. But for people like us, it didn't always move forward. Survival—not comfort—was the only aim.

Especially inside our home, survival was never guaranteed.

In most homes, dinner is a time for sharing stories, laughter, and togetherness. In ours, it was a moment filled with fear.

My mother moved through the kitchen as if she was walking barefoot on shards of glass. Every action was measured—the clang of a spoon, the hiss of the cooker. Even the smell of the food carried tension. Her eyes kept flicking towards the clock. He would arrive any moment now.

My sister Diane and I sat at the dining table, books open in front of us, pretending to study. But our eyes remained fixed on the door. Always the door.

Dinner was always the same—meat, potatoes and some vegetables out of a can. My mother followed routine with precision. Routine gave her the illusion of control, a fragile hope that maybe tonight would pass without any incident.

"Don't speak unless he speaks first," she said in a low voice, smoothing her apron. "And eat quickly." She didn't need to tell us. We already knew.

I gave a slight nod. Diane didn't say a word. Her knuckles were pale as her hands gripped the edge of the table.

Then we heard it—the sound of the car pulling in. The engine turned off then the door slammed shut.

I held my breath.

My mother stood still at the entrance of the kitchen, eyes fixed on the door. Diane and I sat frozen.

The door creaked open. His shoes scraped the floor as he walked in—smelling of alcohol, grease, sweat, and rage.

His shirt was half-unbuttoned, his facial expressions were incomprehensible.

He returned, bringing with him the heavy tension of the day.

My mother stepped forward and placed the food on the table—a hot meal, neatly served.

He first looked at the plate, then at her.

"Hot food?" he snapped. "On a hot day like this?"

"I kept it warm," she replied softly.

But her calm voice was a cold stone against his fury. Without warning, he pushed her to the floor and he was on top of her.

Then, with an eerie tranquility, he fidgeted into the pockets of his pants and pulled out a red-handled knife.

The blade clicked open. The clicking sound echoed through the entire house.

Without a word, he slowly pressed the knife  into her chest.

She didn't scream. Her mouth opened, but the silence swallowed her suffering.

I stood rooted to the spot.

Diane and I looked at each other, both of us in shock, unable to move. For one dreadful moment, I thought we lost her.

Then he got up and walked out of the house, the door slamming behind him.

He went away, probably to the local bar where he liked to drink and flirt with the ladies.

The silence that followed was heavier than any outburst.

She was still breathing—barely.

"We should call the police," I whispered.

"No," she said timidly. "That will only make him more furious."

## Nightfall: Nowhere to Hide

That night, I lay on the bed like a statue, my eyes fixed on the ceiling, straining to hear beyond the silence.

The door slammed. Footsteps thudded—slow, uneven, and very loud. The rhythm was off. Drunken.

I could hear him muttering—slurred and bitter words. He wasn't complaining about anyone but was cursing under his breath. It was a routine; I was accustomed to it very well. He worked at a petrol pump in south Florida, one of those where attendants still pumped fuel, cleaned windscreens, and checked oil. His clothes always carried the stench of engine grease and cheap liquor—as if frustration had soaked deep into the fabric.

This wasn't the life he wanted. And we were the ones who bore the cost.

We had no proper furniture, only plastic garden chairs—meant for patios, not living rooms—lined up like forgotten guests. That was all we could afford. We never called it odd. We just pretended it was normal. Children, after all, are quick to  learn how to lie to themselves when truth hurts too much.

We withstood the punishment of his failures. His drinking worsened. So did the gambling. Whatever little we had vanished into betting slips and poker games. Then he'd return—broke and brutal.

My heart pounded. I could feel each heartbeat echoing in my chest.

And then—the door burst open.

## Living in Imminent Danger

It had been a long time since our house felt like a home. This wasn't a one-time incident. This was our everyday reality.

Anyone raised in a house like mine was knows exactly what "imminent danger" feels like. It's not just a phrase—it's a way of life. It's not only about one violent experience. It's the very air you breathe. It's the silence before the storm. It's the way your body alarms you at every footstep.

We didn't just live with fear—we lived in fear.

The fear was developed in the form of beatings. Sometimes cruel words. Sometimes just a look—cold enough to make your blood thick. Every time, it left a mark. Not always visible, but always there.

## Childhood Stolen, Fear Inherited

At the age of ten, eleven, and twelve—children are supposed to laugh, play in the garden, chase butterflies, or complain about schoolwork. Their days are occupied with sports, cartoons, and dreams of what they want to become.

Me?

I was learning how to become invisible. How to walk without making noise. How to breathe without drawing attention. While others feared a poor score in maths, I feared bruises I couldn't explain.

Marks mattered in my life too—but not the ones on paper. Not the kind from school.

A wrong answer—a slap. A poorly timed word—a beating. Even eye contact—a risk.

It was the kind of silence that smothered you—tight in your chest, cold on your skin. Your heartbeat slowed. But the fear pulsed louder.

The beatings were constant, several times a week.

"Bend over. Touch your toes," he commanded.

Those were not just instructions. They were sentences. The punishment had already been decided.

"I obeyed. I always obeyed." I repeated in a dread.

The belt struck. Pain flared up my spine. I gasped—sometimes in silence, sometimes in screams.

Another strike. CRACK.

"You think you can take it?"

Again. And again.

There was no pattern. No logic. He stopped only when he felt like it—not when the pain was immense.

Then—just like that—he would walk away. As if nothing had happened.

While other children were deciding  which game to play after school …while I was calculating how to survive.

I used to watch other kids coming home—calling for their mothers, giggling, carefree. Their homes looked like havens. I wondered what that must feel like—to be loved, to feel safe. I didn't know any of that.

Did the neighbours know? Of course, they did. The walls were thin. Our house echoed with shrilling voices, crashing furniture, the kind of shrieking sobs that could never be fully hidden. The sharp crack of glass breaking—followed by the silence that echoed.

But no one came to our rescue. No knocks. No inquiries. No police calls. Just silence.

Sometimes, the worst cruelty is not what people do to you—but what they allow to happen.

And he ensured we remained silent.

"If you ever tell anyone, I'll kill you," he threatened.

It wasn't a threat. We knew he meant it. We had seen what he was capable of.

So we stayed silent.

## Education: My Escape

In a world that made no sense, education became my only sanctuary. When everything around me felt like it could fall apart any moment, books were the one place I found order. A maths problem had a solution. Grammar had rules. History had reasons. Maths had formulas that made sense.

There was no sense of fear between the pages. No belts. No terror. In that world, I could breathe. And little by little, I began to rewrite my own future.

But the road ahead wasn't easy.

When I was twelve, my parents divorced. He ran off with his best friend's wife, leaving behind a mountain of debt. In those days, in America, it was nearly impossible for a woman to own property without a man's signature. And my mother—already broken in body and spirit—had to begin from scratch.

We had almost nothing. She applied for welfare. We survived on food stamps—those little coloured slips of paper that we tore off carefully at the grocery store. I remember watching her do it, with her eyes cast down, trying not to draw attention. Yet, she carried herself with dignity, even when the world gave her no reason to.

Each day was a calculation.

How long could we stretch the consumption of milk? Could dinner be made from yesterday's leftovers?

There were nights she didn't eat. She would say she wasn't hungry, but we knew she was saving food for us.

Survival was her full-time job. She had no time. No money. No support.

She was determined that our story should not end the way hers did. So she sacrificed.

## A Turning Point

It was during one of our difficult years that everything changed.

Tired of working at low-paying jobs, my mother decided to go back to college. A bold step for any woman—let alone one with children, no money, and no safety net.

There was only one problem. The college was across a dangerous neighbourhood. She didn't feel safe driving through it alone at night. So she took me along.

I used to sit at the back of her classroom, doing my homework. Scribbling notes. Reading anything I could find.

One evening, the professor approached me. He peered over his glasses at me.

"If you're going to sit in my class, you might as well try to follow along," he said.

Then he handed me an algebra book.

That moment changed everything.

I opened the book and began solving problems—one after the other. I didn't stop.

Within three weeks, I had completed the entire semester's syllabus.

The professor was stunned.

He handed me the advanced level book. I finished that too.

Then, one evening after class, he took my mother aside to discuss something.

"Your son is gifted," he told her.

She smiled—a strained smile, full of both pride and pain.

"I'd like him to enrol here," he said.

She hesitated. "We can't afford that."

The professor was silent for a moment. Then he said softly, "You don't have to. I've already arranged a full scholarship for him."

Just like that, the path of my life changed. By the time I completed ninth grade, I had already finished calculus, degree-level English, and Spanish.

I skipped the tenth grade altogether. For the first time, I saw the road ahead clearly—not as something to survive, but as something to shape.

## A Void That Nothing Could Fill

I was fifteen when my father ended his life.

Officially, it was called an accident—"the gun went off while he was cleaning it." But in my heart, I knew it wasn't an accident. It was his final act of surrender.

We received a call one evening. A heavy voice on the other end of the line.

"Eddie... your father's gone."

Gone.

I thought they meant he'd left. Again. Like he used to. "He's dead. A gunshot."

I froze, tears streaming down my face. My breath hitched.

I called my mother. She didn't react. Her voice was flat.

"Oh," she said. "I'll be right home."

She arrived soon after. Her face—pale. Her eyes—swollen, but dry. She sat quietly.

Jay—my closest friend—was with me for support.

At the funeral, the truth came out.

He had taken his own life.

People murmured, "He was troubled … a broken man…"

But no one asked about the broken family he left behind.

What about us? His pain is over, but ours continues.

His violence didn't end with him. His absence didn't negate the years of damage. The bruises faded—the scars remained.

Some people cried at the funeral. Others stared at the floor. I felt everything—relief, sadness, freedom, and a strange hollowness.

The man who had been both our father and tormentor was gone. But his shadow remained. Even then, I knew—it would stay with me for years.

## Finding Freedom Through Education

I graduated near the top of my class—eighth out of 800 and completed my associate degree that same week.

I should have felt proud—and to some extent, I did.

Yet pride was accompanied by deep emptiness.

Yes, I had escaped. I had made it out—yet the weight of survival still clung to me.

In 1976, at the age of seventeen, I joined the university as a third-year student and chose accounting as my major. It was the first time I stepped into a future no longer ruled by fear.

For once, I wasn't "the boy from that broken home." I could start fresh—be someone new.

Campus felt like another planet—open, alive, and full of possibility. People laughed freely. The gardens were full of colours, the lawns alive with music. I found it easy to make friends. It appeared on the surface that  I blended in. I was thriving.

But inside—I still held back.

Trusting someone wasn't easy for me. I had learned early that it could be broken in an instant.

Jay was by my side the entire time. My closest friend since I was nine, he kept reminding me of where I had come from, and how far I still had to go. He was the only one who knew the full story.

Academics gave  structure to my life—routine, stability. Every subject, every exam, every discussion in class—was one more step away from the frightened child I had once been.

I drowned myself in studies and made some friends. To the world, I was just another college student chasing a bright future. Deep inside, the wounds were still raw. Healing hadn't begun. I was just hiding the pain beneath layers of ambition.

Financial pressure was constant.

To survive, I worked. Library assistant during the day. Bookkeeper at a travel agency at night. Later, I picked up jobs as a bartender and income tax preparer. I needed the income—to afford textbooks, meals, and rent.

I was always tired. Always rushing from one thing to the next.

But maybe … that was the plan.

If I stayed busy enough, I wouldn't have time to feel deeply.

My dorm room was small, but it was mine. The one space where I didn't have to pretend. Where I didn't have to explain myself to anyone.

But my real escape was the library.

Surrounded by shelves of dusty books and under the soft flicker of yellow lights, I would study late into the night. There, in that silence, I imagined a different life—a life where fear no longer chased me.

The past didn't leave me yet, it found ways to sneak in.

Sometimes, while reading, I'd hear his voice in my head— sharp, mocking.

"You're useless!" my mind recalled his words.

My chest would tighten. My pulse would race.

Even though I had left the house, and he had left this world, the haunting memories stayed.

Jay would try to reassure me. "You're not that boy anymore, Eddie. You made it out."

I'd nod. Smile. But inside, I knew the truth.

I was still wearing the same mask—the one I had crafted to survive.

At university, I created a new identity—full of energy, optimism, and success. I convinced myself that if I kept moving fast, my past couldn't catch me.

But it always did.

At times, I sought escape—too often—in things I shouldn't have. Anything to hush the thoughts. To make the noise inside quiet.

The past did not let go easily.

It crept into my dreams. In one of the dreams, he came back to me with his eyes cold, his words echoing, "you're useless" over and over.

Would I ever truly be free?

Every morning, I asked myself that same question.

Education became—my oxygen, my way out.

But freedom is never just about walking away from a place. It's about learning to carry the pain—without letting it carry you. And that part—was still ahead of me.

## A Summer in the Foothills

That summer I travelled to the foothills of the Appalachians, surrounded by tall trees and quiet skies. For someone raised in the rough corners of South Florida, it was the first time I had seen life slow down.

For Indian readers, it was like stepping from the clamour of a crowded street into the stillness of the Western Ghats— green, serene, and oddly unfamiliar.

My uncle died when I was small. His wife, who I called Aunt Audre, had remarried. Her home held a warmth I'd never known. It felt strange, this steadiness.

She was sharp-tongued, soft-hearted—the sort who would scold you for being late and then make your favourite snack without saying a word.

When I arrived, she wrapped me in a hug.

"Eddie, I'm so glad you're here," she said. "We've a lot to talk about."

Her house took my breath away: a long drive, gardens rolling to the horizon, a pool that shimmered in sunlight. Yet it wasn't the house that changed me—it was her.

Even in safety, my body stayed alert, braced for danger. Slowly, day by day, I began to exhale. We spent time with my cousins, but the truest moments were with her—the talks, the way she looked at me as if I mattered.

## Speaking the Unspoken

One evening we sat in the kitchen, bottles of chilled Coca-Cola between us. She leaned forward.

"Eddie… How are you coping with your father's death?"

I froze. No one had ever asked.

"I don't know," I whispered. "I don't think I've let myself think about it."

She waited, saying nothing, and that silence let me speak.

"He was always angry," I said. "Every night—drinking, gambling, shouting, beating us. He'd waste what we had, then punish us for it. You never knew what might set him off."

Her hands clenched. "How did your mother let that happen?"

"She was broken," I said. "He kept her isolated, threatened her. He said he'd kill us if we told anyone, and we believed him."

Her anger softened to sorrow. "I'm sorry," she whispered. "That no one stopped him."

"We were invisible," I said. "Or people saw and looked away."

She swallowed hard. "He should've rotted in jail. Dying was too easy."

We sat for a long time in silence. Then she said words I still carry:

"You are not what he did to you. You're a good person, Eddie."

Tears slipped down my face—quiet, steady.

"I thought if I achieved enough," I said, "I could erase it all."

"You don't need to be someone else," she said softly. "You already are someone—and stronger than you know."

She didn't try to fix me. Her words simply held me, and for the first time, I let myself be held.

## Safe for the First Time

That summer, the nightmares eased. I slept deeply, peacefully. In the hush of the hills, beneath early light, I changed.

I felt safe—truly safe. When I left, I wasn't the same. I still carried my memories, yet also a fragile belief that healing was possible.

For years I tried to outrun pain, thinking success would make me whole. It never did. Healing came not from achievement but from being seen and heard—a lesson I learned slowly, over decades.

And far away, decades later, a young girl was beginning her own journey—stepping onto a train, leaving everything she knew behind for a life that promised nothing, except change.

# Chapter 3

# Our New Life in Hyderabad

I had no idea what awaited us in Hyderabad. I was just a girl being taken to the city, uncertain whether I was leaving behind everything I knew or stepping into the entirely unknown.

When Amma left for Hyderabad the first time, she went alone—determined to earn enough to support our growing needs. Until then, Nana's tailoring had been enough to carry us through. He stitched clothes for people in our village and nearby towns. But when Jyothi and I started school, the expenses increased—books, uniforms, bus fare—and Amma stepped forward.

She found work through one of the acquaintances, and soon she was employed by a woman called Raji Madam in Hyderabad. She cooked, cleaned, and did whatever was needed in exchange for a wage and a place to stay. Sometimes we'd get a message through a neighbor's phone or a handwritten note delivered by a cousin: "I'm okay. Be good, girls. I miss you both."

After nearly a year, we were joining Amma. But it wasn't Amma who came to fetch us—it was our grandmother.

"Pack only what you need," Avva, my grandmother, said that morning, rolling up our clothes tightly into little bundles. "The train will be loaded. We don't want to lose anything." She tied everything in her old cotton sari, turned into a makeshift sack.

I was sitting cross-legged on the floor, nervously pulling at the hem of my faded kurta. "Avva … how will we know where to go? Hyderabad is very large, no?"

She looked at me over the rim of her glasses, her forehead creased with concern, but her voice steady. "I have the address. Your Amma wrote it for me. And this," she said, pulling a crumpled paper from the folds of her blouse, "a landline number. Once we get there, we'll call."

Jyothi stood near the doorway, clutching her small metal lunch box tightly. "Will Amma meet us at the station?"

"She can't take leave from work," Avva said. "But don't worry. When we call after reaching there, someone will come."

We left Boyalakuntla before dawn. The sky was still deep blue, and a thin layer of mist hung low over the fields. Avva carried everything—food, clothes, a blanket rolled under her arm. Jyothi and I walked side by side, silent, trying not to show our fear.

## On the Train

At the station, we watched the train arrive—huge, noisy, breathing out steam like a living creature. The engine gave out a sharp, screeching cry, and its headlights glared like fierce eyes in the dim morning. The metal steps were glistened with dew, and the coach inside smelt like steel, damp earth, and a waft of something fried—maybe *vadas* from someone's tiffin.

We squeezed into a corner near the window. Jyothi sat beside me, knees pulled up, toes peeking from under her skirt. I leaned into Avva's soft side, trying to act brave, though my stomach felt tight like a knotted thread.

"Are we still in Andhra, Avva?" I asked, a little while after the train began moving.

She chuckled softly and patted my leg. "Yes, we are. Hyderabad is in Andhra too—only expansive, different. You'll understand when we reach."

At that time, it was true—Hyderabad was a part of Andhra Pradesh. It was only years later, in 2014, that Telangana became a separate state and Hyderabad was declared its capital. But back then, to us, it was just the big city where Amma had gone—a place filled with lights, buses, English-speaking people, and things we couldn't yet imagine.

Outside the window, the world rolled past in long strips—green, gold, and brown. Fields of cotton and sunflower stretched out on both sides, their heads bowed with dew. We passed banana groves, thorny bushes, and patches of sugarcane, all blurred together like strokes of a giant paintbrush. Cows and goats grazed near the tracks, skinny and slow-moving, their bones jutting dusty skin.

Near Cumbum, the train slowed down next to a wide, shimmering lake—one of those old tanks built long ago by kings, Avva said. Mist rose from the surface, and fishermen stood knee-deep, casting nets with slow, trained arms. Beyond, the Nallamala Hills looked bluish and gentle, half-hidden in morning haze.

Children stood near the tracks, waving with both hands. Some ran barefoot on the red mud, and others sat on oversized bicycles. Old women in faded saris squatted outside huts, cooking over open fires that fumed up streams of smoke.

The train stopped at every small town station—Dhone, Kurnool, Gadwal. At each stop, the platform bustled with movement. Tea vendors called out, "Chai, chai, hot chai!" balancing steel kettles over their shoulders. A man walked past carrying boiled peanuts in a cone of newspaper. Another shouted, "Bajjis! Mirchi bajjis! (green chilli fritters!)" while the smell of fried green chillies drifted through the carriage.

It rocked us like a cradle—its rhythm constant. We opened the banana-leaf package Avva had brought from home—three idlis pressed together with a dollop of coconut chutney smeared on top. The chutney had soaked into the leaf, and everything smelled faintly of mustard seeds and curry leaves. It was cold but comforting. Jyothi picked her share. I ate mine fast, more to keep from trembling than out of hunger.

"Do you think Amma will look different?" Jyothi asked suddenly.

"Why should she?" I replied, wiping my mouth.

"She's in the city now. Maybe she wears different saris. Maybe she learned English."

Avva didn't say anything at first. Then she reached out and tenderly brushed our hair, one hand on each of our heads, as though reminding us we were still the same.

As we neared Hyderabad, the landscape began to change. The trees grew fewer. Tall buildings appeared between stretches of scrubland. Instead of bullock carts, we saw lorries—huge trucks painted in bold colours with slogans like "Horn OK Please" and "Use Dipper at Night". The streets were crammed with life—laundry hung from windows like flags, and shops were squeezed close together, spilling vegetables and plastic buckets onto the roadside.

The sky had turned a hazy orange by the time we reached the outskirts. By the time we passed Mahbubnagar, everything moved faster—cars, buses, people. The train, too, seemed to pick up speed—it was no longer just chugging.

We arrived in Hyderabad just as the sun dipped behind the buildings. The station was louder than anything I had ever known. Porters yelling at one another. Wheels clattering on platforms. Families shouted greetings or goodbyes. Stray dogs sniffing the  spilled food around. The air was thick with the smell of oil, sweat, and something sweet—probably jalebis frying in a stall nearby.

We stood near the station wall, holding our bundles tightly and looking around, not sure where to go. Then suddenly Avva gasped and clutched at her waist. Her eyes went wide.

"Our bags," she said. "They're gone."

We spun around. Everything—our clothes, the old books, even the small steel box with our combs and soaps—had vanished. Someone had taken them in the crowd, silent as a shadow.

She didn't shout. She didn't panic. Her lips pressed together, her jaw set firm. Then she stood up straight, took a deep breath, and slipped her hand in the blouse. She took out a crumpled piece of paper, carefully folded.

"Come," she said. "We'll call now."

We went to make a call—inside the small glass booth, the air was hot and it was filled with the smell of rusted coins and cigarette smoke. She inserted the coin in the slot and pressed the telephone buttons with her rough, steady fingers. The phone—black, rang loudly against the city's cacophony.

Once. Twice.

Then: "Hello?"

Avva's voice cracked slightly, but she held it together. "This is Mahalakshmi's mother. We have arrived. We're at the station."

There was a beat of silence. Then we could hear Amma's voice—relieved, breathless. "Amma! You brought them? Are they safe? I'm coming now. Don't move from there!"

Avva hung up and looked at us. "She's coming."

And she did.

Less than an hour later, Amma was there—breathless, her braid loose, her eyes darting until they found us. Her face broke open into a smile the moment she saw us, and she ran forward, embracing us both in her arms.

"Na papa… na bangaru… my girls," she whispered, pressing her forehead to ours. "You've come. You're safe."

Next she turned to her mother. The two of them didn't speak—just locked eyes for a moment. Their connection was forged in silence, a testament to everything they had been through together.

We didn't have our bags. We didn't have clean clothes. But at that moment, none of it mattered.

We had Amma.

And that was enough.


## Our New Home… Or So I Thought

We entered through the front gate.

Amma led us around the side to the back, past a long row of freshly washed clothes dancing in the wind. A jute sack leaking rice lay against the wall. The back wasn't like the front—it was more narrow.

"This is our room," Amma said, her hand resting on the latch of a worn wooden door.

Inside, it was dim and plain. The room had minimal essentials: a rolled mattress, a clay water pot in the corner, and a small shelf stacked with soap, hair oil, and a few utensils. No window. Just four walls and a ceiling that echoed with the noise of the kitchen on the floor above ours.

Jyothi stood beside me, taking a glance at the room. "So… we live here? Inside Madam's house but… not really?"

Amma didn't answer immediately. She bent down and started untying the corners of a small cloth bundle, spreading out a couple of folded clothes.

"It's not much, but it is safe," she finally said.

I nodded, but my chest felt tight. This wasn't what I had imagined when I heard the word city. Not this tucked-away space behind someone else's house. Not this borrowed corner of someone else's life.

Later that evening, Amma gave us a quick tour of what she called "our area." The bathroom was outside, attached to a tiny courtyard, just little wider than a doorway.

Just the thought of stepping half-asleep into that frigid stone yard for a bath gave me goosebumps.

"What if someone sees us?" Jyothi asked, clutching her dupatta tightly.

"No one will," Amma replied gently. "I always finish before Madam wakes. You should also do the same."

There was no space for protest. Just silence.

## The First Night

That night, I couldn't sleep.

The mattress was thin and coarse. The room felt hot and airless, like the walls were pressing in on us. I missed the cool night breeze of our village, the way the wind rustled through neem trees outside our window, the smell of earth after rain. Here, it smelled like steel, cooked onions, and the strange perfume Madam used.

I realised  as Amma's breathing slowed. She was asleep. Jyothi shifted beside me, pulling the sheet closer to her neck.

"Devi," she whispered, "are you awake?"

"Mm-hmm."

"I can't sleep."

"Me neither."

We lay still in the dark.

"I keep thinking about Nandyal," she said. "I even miss the frogs croaking near the well."

I swallowed the lump rising in my throat. "I miss everything. Even the rough floor at Avva's house felt better than this."

Jyothi rolled toward me, her voice feeble now. "Do you think we'll get to study here?"

"I don't know," I whispered. "But I'm keeping my books with me, just in case."

She reached out and touched my hand. We stayed that way—two sisters holding hands in the dark, trying to be brave for a world that wasn't ready to be kind.

## Running Water

The next morning, Amma took us to the bathroom and turned a knob below the sink. Water rushed out—clear, cold, and endless.

I gasped. "Jyothi! Look water!"

She came running—eyes wide. "It's not a hand pump?"

"No," I said, letting the water trickle through my fingers. "It just… comes. From the wall!"

We stared—half in awe, half in disbelief. Amma opened the tap in the shower. More water. Then she flushed the toilet. Even that worked without pouring a mug from a bucket.

We cherished it like we had discovered gold.

Jyothi shouted. "No more carrying pots!"

I splashed some on my face. It was icy and thrilling. My whole body shivered, but I didn't stop. After years of drawing water from a neighbour's well, of balancing it on our heads, of counting every drop—we finally had water we didn't have to beg for.

Amma smiled faintly as she watched us, like she had been waiting for this moment all along.

## This Wasn't Home… Not Yet

Still, something felt off. The water flowed. The room had walls. The city sparkled just beyond the gate. But it didn't feel like ours.

I missed knowing the names of every neighbor. I missed the familiar dust of our street, the rhythm of people who waved when they passed. Here, no one greeted us. No one noticed us. It was as if we existed between the cracks—visible only to each other.

At night, I pressed my schoolbooks to my chest like a shield.

I remembered my teacher back in Nandyal. She once touched my shoulder and said, "You are smart, Devi. Don't stop learning, no matter where you go."

I whispered those words to myself like a prayer.

Even if this room never became home... maybe school could be.

# Chapter 4

# Running Hard, Standing Still

That summer in the foothills gave me my first taste of peace—not just freedom from harm, but freedom to truly feel. I had always believed survival was the goal. But in those days, I began to see that healing was different altogether. It wasn't about forgetting the past—it was about no longer letting it control me.

When I left, I carried more than just memories. I carried a fragile hope that, perhaps, I could also live a life free from fear—a life I could shape for myself. As I returned to Florida and stepped back into the whirlwind of studies, work, and expectations, I realised how easily it was to slip back into old habits. The world demanded constant movement. I responded by speeding up. The world expected strength. I responded by burying my pain deeper.

I thought I had escaped. But the truth was, I had only changed the form of my prison.

I no longer studied just to survive; I studied to disappear. Success became my shield. Every achievement was another affirmation that I was okay—when I wasn't.

## Lessons from the Bar and the Ledger

Returning to the University of Florida was jarring. Gone were the gentle conversations and steady support—replaced by pressure and pace. I had two years left in the university, and survival came at a cost.

I did multiple jobs. One was bartending—a common part of American college life. Behind the counter, I served strangers who were trying to forget their pain while silently carrying my own. Later, I switched to tax preparation—drawn to the logic and structure. Numbers didn't lie. They don't hurt you. They just made sense.

I kept pushing—to prove I could make it. But over time, I couldn't tell where the performance ended and I began.

At the age of twenty, I moved to Florida's capital, Tallahassee, and became a district manager for a tax firm—leading eighteen offices and hundreds of people. On paper, I was working in a tax firm. Inside, I still questioned everything. Can I really do this? Am I enough?

Each day tested me—professionally and personally. I was learning to lead while still battling the voices inside my head that told me I didn't belong.

## There Was Still No Escape

I shifted my career to teaching and later began working for IBM when desktops computers came out in the 1980s. That role took me from Florida to New York. Yet, no matter how far I had come or what I had achieved, the weight of my past seemed to trail behind me, always threatening to pull me back. I presented a facade of control, even when I wasn't in control, convincing myself that professional success would somehow erase the inner turmoil. Deep down, I knew that no title, no position, could overcome the pain I had buried so deeply inside me.

In the midst of this, I found comfort in teaching and mentoring. Helping others in the growing field of technology gave me a sense of purpose—a momentary reprieve from my battles. Training someone in a new skill, guiding a junior colleague, allowed me to connect with others, while  my own struggles remained unresolved. But a fear lingered: was I truly healing, or was I just learning to hide my wounds better?

Still, no matter how much I achieved, a darkness gnawed at me from within. The cycle of harm didn't end just because the abuse had stopped.

Instead of confronting my pain, I tried to bury it. The only control I had was over my own self-destruction. I binged on food—eating recklessly to suppress the turmoil in my mind. I turned to intense workouts at the gym. Hour after hour, I pushed my body to its limits—lifting weights until my muscles ached, sprinting on the treadmill until my lungs burned. For a while, physical exhaustion drowned out the emotional pain. But once I stopped, the memories and self-doubt returned— stronger than ever.

Isolation became my way of life. I withdrew from friends, and avoided social events, only allowing others to see me at work or in the gym. Despite my progress, I still feared I wasn't enough—that I hadn't truly reached where I wanted to.

It took years for me to understand how my silence and self-destructive habits only strengthened the cycle. My father's abuse had set it in motion; society's indifference had allowed it to fester. My own refusal to confront my pain—wrapped in shame and secrecy—had given it the space to thrive. Only when I finally acknowledged my wounds and allowed myself to be vulnerable did I begin breaking free. That was the true power of recognising the cycle: it was the first step towards unravelling it.

## Meeting My Life Partner: A Love Built on Resilience

My life took a new turn when I met Pris. I stood on the edge of a meaningful future and still I clung to the mask I had perfected over the years. I had become an expert at hiding my wounds, showing only the parts of me I wanted the world to see. She saw the version of me I had carefully constructed—a man who had moved past his struggles, who carried himself with confidence. I was determined not to let my past interfere with what we were building. No matter how much I tried to keep my distance, something about her made it difficult to keep my walls intact.

Ours was a love forged through resilience. Pris wasn't just my partner; she was my anchor, the steady presence who grounded me when the echoes of my past threatened to pull me under. She never tried to erase my pain or assume that love alone could heal everything. Instead, she walked beside me, offering strength and unwavering support, giving me the space to confront my inner demons at my own pace. Together, we built a life that wasn't defined by the scars we carried, but by the commitment we made to each other.

No matter how much love surrounded me, it wasn't enough to undo the years of conditioning. I carried my past like an invisible weight, even when I longed to let it go. No matter how many friends I had, how successful I became, or how deeply Pris loved me, I never truly allowed myself to take off the mask.

My career took off. I joined a leading global consulting firm known for helping governments and businesses navigate complex strategic and technological challenges. Between 1998 and 2005, I led the development of their corporate university, turning it into a globally recognised centre for learning and leadership. It earned praise and awards from all over the world.

From the outside, everything appeared perfect. I was travelling across countries, leading top-performing teams, speaking at international conferences, and mentoring future leaders. My network grew, our children grew, and professionally I was considered successful. I had mastered the art of achievement—the posture, the polish, the composure expected of someone who had "made it."

Yet inside, nothing had truly changed. I wore my success like a suit of armour—gleaming, strong, and precisely fitted—convincing everyone around me that I had left my past behind. The truth was far less heroic. I had not escaped it. I had only hidden it better.

The mask I wore fooled everyone. It never slipped—not during award ceremonies, not in boardrooms, not at family gatherings, and certainly not in the quiet hours of the night when I should have felt safe enough to exhale. With time, the mask did not simply cover my face; it fused with me. I could no longer tell where the performance ended and the person began.

I was respected, yes—admired even—yet in many ways, I remained invisible. The truth was that I had never allowed myself to feel safe without the mask. Beneath the calm exterior lived a constant fear: that if I ever removed it, I would be exposed, vulnerable, and somehow unworthy of the life I had built. So I continued the act, rehearsed and seamless, convincing the world and, most dangerously, convincing myself.

Even when love entered my life, even as my children grew and my friendships deepened, I kept the past locked away—buried beneath layers of competence and control. I told myself that strength meant silence, that healing meant moving on. Yet the past does not vanish simply because it is unspoken. It waits—patient, persistent, and certain.

It reappears in the moments between applause and exhaustion, in the hollowness that follows achievement, in the ache that lingers when the world believes you are thriving. It whispers through the fatigue of holding everything together and the weight of pretending to be fine.

Then, in 2003, my mother—who had suffered alongside us, who loved me deeply and whom I loved in return—passed away. Our relationship had always been layered, tender and turbulent in equal measure. She was the one constant presence through the chaos of my childhood, the quiet force who carried us when there was no one else to turn to. Yet even as an adult, part of me still carried the anguish of a child who had not been protected.

I knew she had endured her own torment. I had seen the fear in her eyes, the weariness in her movements, the silence she used as armour when survival demanded it. I understood, intellectually, that she had done what she could—that leaving was not simple, that fear can trap even the strongest hearts. Yet another part of me—the small boy who had hidden from his father's rage—still longed for her to have done more, to have taken us away, to have saved us.

When she died, those contradictions flooded back with a force I could not contain. Grief was not a single emotion; it was an ache made of love and loss, sorrow and fury, forgiveness and longing. I missed her terribly—her warmth, her humour, the gentle way she called my name—and at the same time, I felt the old wounds reopening, sharper for never having been spoken aloud.

In her final years, we had grown close. There were long conversations, shared memories, and moments of quiet understanding. Yet beneath the closeness, something remained unsaid—the unhealed distance between mother and son, built not from a lack of love, but from the weight of what we had both survived. When she was gone, I realised that the chance to untangle those knots had gone with her.

Her death unsettled the fragile balance I had built. It drew the past out of hiding, forcing me to confront not only what had been done to us, but also what had never been said between us. It was as though the silence I had spent my life maintaining suddenly had an echo. And in that echo, the boy I had buried began to stir.

In the months that followed, I threw myself deeper into work. I travelled even more, filled every space in my diary, and surrounded myself with motion. Movement had always been my way of staying ahead of the silence. If I kept going, I would not have to listen to the echoes. If I kept achieving, no one—not even I—would question what was missing.

Grief, however, does not respect schedules. It waits in the pauses—between flights, between meetings, between one version of myself and the next. It found me in hotel rooms after midnight, in airport lounges where faces blurred and memories returned. I would sit surrounded by comfort and success and still feel a familiar emptiness settling in, like mist creeping through a closed window.

I began to sense the exhaustion of living two lives—the one the world applauded and the one I kept hidden. The more I tried to separate them, the heavier they became. Yet still, I told myself that this was what resilience looked like: composure, control, and constant motion.

There were moments—fleeting and uninvited—when I would catch my reflection and not fully recognise the man staring back. The eyes looked confident, the smile assured, yet behind them lived a restlessness I could not quiet. I told myself it was fatigue, the cost of ambition. It was easier to believe that than to admit what I already knew: that success had become my mask, and the silence behind it was growing louder.

I continued to lead, to speak, to deliver, to inspire—and outwardly, nothing seemed amiss. Yet beneath the surface, a quiet unease began to build, subtle but constant, like a low hum I could not switch off. By the early months of 2005, I had everything I had ever worked for—stability, recognition, and the trappings of a life well lived. Yet in the stillness between moments, I felt an ache I could no longer name. Something was stirring beneath the armour, though I could not yet see what it was.

## The First Crack in the Mask

Then, in early 2005, a new opportunity came my way.

I was invited to speak to a group of adults graduating from a welfare-to-work programme. These were individuals who had faced immense hardship—poverty, abuse, loss—and yet, here they were, ready to begin a new chapter in their lives. The name of the organisation was Training Futures, and Booz Allen was one of its proud sponsors.

I agreed to speak, not realising how much that day would move me.

As I looked out at them, I understood that this moment wasn't only about me. My story, my words—they belonged to everyone who had struggled and survived. Everyone who still carried hope in their hearts.

I spoke about a woman—her strength, her sacrifices, and the love that never left her, even in her final days. I ended my speech with these words:

> Ladies and gentlemen, you all know the courage it takes to reach out for help because each of you has done the same.
>
> You took that first step when you joined Training Futures—that was your first act of bravery.
>
> Your second courageous and well-earned step is what you are achieving today, graduating from Training Futures.
>
> The third step is to find a job and keep it. Yes, there will always be another step ahead, and sometimes it may feel as if you are not moving forward fast enough.
>
> But as I told you today about who learned that life is a continuous journey. Training Futures and your accomplishments here will not make life perfect but, I am certain they will make it better. As you move forward, I hope you will remember the story I'm sharing with you—the story of a woman

who, after years of suffering and hardship, reached out for help, lifted herself up, and built a new life for herself and her family. And in doing so, she inspired a child to dream bigger than she could have ever imagined.

I stand before you today as the next generation. And today, I am here representing your sons, your daughters, and all the children whose lives you will shape through your journey.

For your future, and for the future of your next generation, I wish you all the very best on this path. And most importantly, I thank you for having the courage to take that journey.

For a moment, the audience was completely silent. Perhaps they were surprised that a senior executive—someone who had travelled across the world and built a successful career—was now standing before them, sharing such personal and painful truths. And then, almost as if breaking free from some invisible restraint, they all stood up and applauded.

Speaking about my lived experiences did not bring the relief I had imagined. Instead of feeling free, I felt exposed. As I opened up my wounds to others, they also reopened inside me. Pain that had been buried for so long—so deep that even I had begun to believe it was gone—suddenly returned. My voice trembled, my heart pounded, and as I stepped away from the stage, I felt more vulnerable than I ever had before.

The next speaker was visibly emotional. He struggled to begin, and then he turned towards me—his voice thick with emotion, and thanked me for my courage. I wanted to shrink, to disappear. But I stood firm. For far too long, I had carried the weight of silent shame. That day, I decided it was time to face it. I wanted to honour my mother. I wanted her to be proud of me.

That speech wasn't just a talk—it was a reckoning with my past. Until then, I had lived behind a mask, one that I had worn so convincingly that even I had started to believe in its strength. But while speaking those words, I felt that mask begin to crack. The layers of it cracked in ways that made me uncomfortable. I wasn't ready to take it off completely, but for the first time, I became aware of just how heavy it had been all these years.

Even then, I did not have the courage to speak directly in the first person. The pain still felt too raw, too personal. So, I shared my mother's story in the third person—as if that bit of emotional distance would help me say what I could not yet own fully as mine.

Still, something changed inside me that day. Even though I wasn't ready to embrace full vulnerability, I had taken the first step. That speech marked a turning point. The mask— once firm and unyielding, had started to slip. And in that moment of raw honesty, I caught a glimpse of what I had never allowed myself to believe—perhaps, one day, I could let it go completely.

## Our Move to India: A New Path

In late 2005, we were offered an opportunity to join a rapidly growing tech company in India. Pris and I made a decision that would change the course of our lives. It wasn't just about work or seeking adventure. It was about leaving behind the familiar, stepping out of our comfort zone, and trying to release the weight of a past that seemed to follow me, no matter how far I went.

One evening, we called MacKenzie into the living room for a chat. She was fifteen at that time, and we knew what we were about to share would turn her world upside down. We told her about going to India and explained that it was a chance for a fresh start, a new chapter—for all three of us.

MacKenzie—naturally—had questions. "Why India?" she asked. "Why so far away?"

Pris tried to reassure her. "We feel it's the right step for us. It's not just about going to a new place—it's about growth. About experiencing the world together."

At first, she looked stunned. Who wouldn't be? But as we spoke, her expression slowly began to change. The idea was difficult, yes—but there was also a flicker of curiosity, of adventure, in her eyes.

We had no idea then, but while we were preparing to step into a completely new phase of life, far across the globe, a young girl was entering a new chapter of her own.

Very soon, our worlds would meet—and neither of us would ever be the same again.

# Part 2
# Unlikely Paths Cross

"When you want something, all the universe conspires in helping you to achieve it."

—Paulo Coelho, *The Alchemist*

# Chapter 5

# Support at Unexpected Places

When my mother took up work as household help for Raji Madam, I had just entered eighth standard. Everything changed so quickly, I didn't know what to think or feel.

The new colony wasn't like the one we had left behind. Here, order ruled everything—from gated compounds to quiet afternoons. The houses were bigger, freshly painted, and had well-maintained gardens with actual grass instead of patches of bare soil. Even the roads were wide and neatly paved, lined with young trees. Everything here felt planned—neat footpaths, trimmed hedges, and iron gates marking each home.

The chinna (small) outhouse behind Raji Madam's bungalow, where we now stayed, was still just a single room with a bathroom outside. But it was neat, and somehow, it felt better than what we were used to.

## A World Under Construction

New homes were still being built all around us. The air was filled with the strong smell of wet cement and fresh paint, mixing with the dusty scent of drying mud. Stacks of bricks, heaps of sand, and iron rods lay scattered along the roadside, waiting to be used. Each morning began with the clang of hammers and the *dhak-dhak* of chisels, ringing out across the colony like a call to begin. Every now and then, a whistle rang out, followed by shouts while *mazdoors* (labourers) took instructions from the constructor overseeing the work.

By mid-afternoon, the sun scorched the half-finished houses, heating the dust in the air, making it cling to the workers' sweaty skin. Their faces—smeared with white cement dust—were barely visible beneath their sweat-drenched *rumals* (thin cotton towels) as they carried heavy loads on their heads.

These workers did not live inside the colony. They parked their cycles and scooters outside the main gates or arrived by bus, walking the rest of the way in small groups. Their faded shirts stuck to their backs as they crouched to lay tiles or hoisted wooden beams into place. Some wiped their faces with their rumāls, working slowly under the unforgiving afternoon heat.

Despite all this construction, the colony had a certain order to it. The gardens were being planted, young saplings tied to wooden stakes so they would grow straight. Fresh patches of grass had been laid down—still damp from watering. In front of some houses, gardeners carefully sprinkled water from metal cans, pressing the loose mannu (soil) around the roots.

At the entrance, a tall black iron gate stood firm, guarded by two watchmen in khaki uniforms. They sat on plastic chairs inside a small sentry hut, keeping a close eye on everyone passing through. Nobody could enter unless they were a resident or had permission. If a stranger approached, one of the guards would stand up, raise a hand, and demand, "Where are you going?"

We were even stopped by the guards each time—"Whose house?" they would ask, before opening the gate.

This wasn't like our village, where nobody questioned where you went or why. Here, everything had rules—gates, guards, new houses, new roads. It was a world being built—piece by piece—right in front of our eyes.

## Getting to Know Raji Madam

At first, Raji Madam hardly noticed me. She was always busy—giving instructions to Amma, handling household affairs, or sitting with her books and tea. But over time, she started paying attention. She would observe me when I helped Amma, her sharp eyes following my movements around the house.

One afternoon, as I carefully folded the washed clothes, she called me over.

"Devi, do you go to school?" she asked, setting her book aside.

"Yes, Madam," I answered, standing straight. "Eighth standard."

She nodded thoughtfully. "And how are your marks?"

"They are … good, Madam," I replied hesitantly, unsure of what she was thinking.

She studied me for a moment before speaking again. "Education is important, Devi. You must take it seriously."

From that day onwards, Madam started taking interest in me—asking about my studies, my teachers, and what I was learning in school. Sometimes, she would quiz me on English,

Hindi, and Maths in a fun way. She did the same with Jyothi too. She even used to share chocolates with us during break time.

When Jyothi was preparing for her 10th public exams—which, at that time, felt like climbing a mountain—Madam really stepped in. My sister is very quiet and introverted. She doesn't open up easily to anyone. But Madam made her feel safe and comfortable. She taught her with so much patience, in every way she could—explaining again and again until it became clear.

Jyothi cleared her exams because of Madam. And for the first time in years, I saw my sister smile with confidence.

## Raji Madam's Rule

One morning, she called me inside her room. "From today onwards, you will speak to me only in English," she said, folding her hands.

I stared at her. "Madam?"

"If you speak Telugu, I will not answer you. I will pretend I cannot hear you," she said, her voice firm. "If you want to speak with me, you must speak in English. Otherwise, silence."

I felt my stomach drop. How could I manage without Telugu? I only knew a few words in English—enough to say "Yes, Madam" or "No, Madam"—but not enough to have a conversation.

She must have seen the fear on my face when she handed me a notebook. "Start with this," she said. "Every day, write one new word and use it in a sentence. If you make an effort, you will learn."

At first, I thought she was just encouraging me. But she meant it.

That very afternoon, I forgot and spoke in Telugu. "Madam, Amma is asking if—"

She did not even look up and kept reading her book.

I hesitated and tried again. "Madam, Amma is—"

She turned a page, her face blank, as if I wasn't even in the room.

I swallowed. My cheeks burned. I looked at Amma, but she only shook her head, as if to say, it's your mistake. You must follow the rule.

That night, I sat outside, staring at my notebook. I had written one new word earlier, but now, I wrote five. I had no choice—I had to learn.

Raji Madam never scolded me, never raised her voice. But she was strict. If I spoke in Telugu, she would act as if I did not exist.

Every morning, I practiced my sentences before going to her. "Good morning, Madam," I would say, repeating the words in my head first, afraid of making mistakes. She would correct me, but she never let me switch back to Telugu.

"You need discipline," she would say. "And discipline comes from effort, not comfort."

I missed the ease of Telugu. But slowly, the English words stopped feeling so foreign.

## The Driveway Classroom

The driveway became my study place. In the evenings, when the house was noisy with the sounds of utensils clanking and Amma preparing for the next day, I sat outside. Under the dim streetlamp, I spread my books on the ground. It was the only time I could focus properly, without distractions.

"Devi, come inside," Amma called one evening, standing on the doorway. "Your eyes will get weak in this dim light."

"Just a little more time, Amma," I said, not looking up. I needed to finish.

She sighed but did not force me. I think she respected my stubbornness, even if she didn't fully understand it. For Amma, life was about getting through each day. For me, it was about getting out of this life.

Some nights, I studied so late that I fell asleep right there, resting my head on the books. The air in the night was cool and I liked the quietness.

Later, I would learn that I wasn't the only one who had studied under a streetlamp. Dr A.P.J. Abdul Kalam, India's beloved former President, had done the same in his childhood—lighting his path to greatness with nothing but grit—a book and a dim bulb. His story gave me strength. If he could rise from such beginnings, maybe I could too.

Mornings came too fast. The first sunlight would peek over the rooftops, and the city would wake up—the horns of scooters, the chatter of neighbours, and the soft sound of Amma's broom. I would sit up, rub my eyes, and dive back into my books before the day could take me away.

That streetlamp was more than just light—it was hope. It lit up my books and my dreams. The rough cement of the driveway was my classroom—my escape. It wasn't much, but it was enough.

## Foreigners Next Door

For a while, life in the colony remained unchanged. Every morning, the familiar sounds filled the air—the milkman arriving on his cycle, honking twice before dropping off packets at each door; the vegetable vendors calling out the names of fresh sabzi from the street; and the aunties gathered on their balconies, discussing everything from the rising dal prices to the latest serial on TV. Life was predictable, familiar, safe.

Since the homes in our colony were newly built, families moved in as soon as construction was completed. I would watch as each house took shape, brick by brick, wondering what kind of people would live there. Some houses welcomed noisy children who ran around barefoot, some got nosy aunties who always peeped through their windows, and some remained eerily silent.

But nothing could have prepared me for the family that moved in next door.

That afternoon, I was sitting in the courtyard, flipping through my English textbook, underlining difficult words like "exquisite" and "sophisticated." I liked reading, but sometimes, these big words felt unnecessary. Why couldn't they just say "nice" instead of "exquisite"? I was about to close my book when a sudden noise shattered the quiet.

VROOM! VROOM!

I looked up, startled. A convoy of large trucks rumbled down the narrow street—one, two... seven! Right behind them, a sleek, new, tan Honda CRV followed, its polished surface gleaming in the afternoon sun. I had never seen such a fancy car in our colony before. It wasn't like the tiny Maruti cars and aging scooters parked outside most homes.

Curious, I put my book aside and stood up, gripping the iron gate for support. The trucks were packed with furniture, heavy boxes, and even a cycle with thick tyres. They rolled to a stop in front of the empty house beside ours, and the car slid smoothly into the driveway.

Something about it felt different—important.

The first person to step out was the driver, dressed in a spotless white uniform. His movements were precise, disciplined. Without wasting a second, he rushed to open the passenger door. My breath caught as I stared, my fingers tightening around the gate.

A polished black shoe touched the ground first. Then, a tall man stepped out. His trousers were ironed so perfectly that not a single crease showed, and his crisp white shirt looked as if it had never known sweat or dust. His eyes scanned the street—sharp, unreadable. He moved like someone who was used to giving orders rather than taking them.

And then, before I could fully process his presence, another door opened.

A woman stepped out, and I couldn't take my eyes off her.

Her reddish-blonde hair caught the sunlight, glowing like polished copper. She was tall, graceful, and everything about her radiated wealth. In one smooth motion, she removed her sunglasses and surveyed her surroundings. I shrank back slightly, afraid she might notice me staring.

She was unlike any woman I had ever seen in real life. Her dressing sense was different. No sari draped around her, no bangles jingling on her wrists, no dupatta loosely thrown over her shoulder. Instead, she looked like she had stepped straight out of a fashion magazine. Her fitted trousers and stylish top made her seem like an actress from the English films that played on Sunday afternoons.

And then—

Another door opened.

A girl stepped out—older than me. Her long brown hair cascaded down her back in soft waves, and she had large headphones around her neck. Unlike the woman, she wasn't elegant or dramatic. Instead, she was… quiet. Observing. Taking everything in with careful eyes, as if memorising every small detail of the street.

Before I could think too much, a small white dog leaped out of the car, barking happily. I froze.

I had never seen a dog like this before.

The dogs in our area were different. They were bony— so bony their ribs stuck out—and they moved fast, always sniffing around, looking for food. Some limped, others had patches where their fur was missing. They fought near the waste piles, barking and growling over scraps. People ignored them, sometimes shooing them away when they got too close.

But this one… it was small, fluffy, and clean. As if someone had just given it a bath and brushed its fur. It didn't look scary. It wagged its tail and ran in little circles, completely unaware of the kind of life the other dogs lived. It looked… happy. Like it belonged somewhere else.

I didn't have the words for it back then, but the difference between this dog and the ones I was used to seeing felt as vast as the gap between the old city and the gleaming skyscrapers in HITEC City. Same place, but not the same world.

The girl bent down and scooped up the dog, laughing as it licked her cheek. I held my breath.

It was such a simple moment, yet it felt magical—like a scene from one of those foreign books in our school library. A girl and her dog, stepping into a new world together.

I gripped the gate firmly, unable to look away.

Foreigners—I had only seen them on television—on the English movie channels that played on Sunday afternoons or in school textbooks, where fair-skinned people were shown smiling at places that felt as distant as the moon. Their lives always seemed unreal—grand houses, fancy food, big cars. So different from our world—noisy, crowded, and the warm, floury scent of cooking chapatis.

And yet, now, they were here. Right next door.

The man with his commanding presence, the woman with her effortless elegance, the girl with her curiosity—who were they? What kind of life had they lived before coming here? And why did I feel like their arrival was the beginning of something… important?

I was about to take a step forward when—

"Devi!"

Amma's sharp voice cut through the air, making me jump. My hands slipped from the gate.

"Come and help me!"

I turned quickly, my heart still racing. "Yes, Amma," I mumbled, forcing my legs to move. Even as I helped her, my mind stayed outside, stuck on the people next door.

They didn't belong here.

Neither did I.

Maybe that's why I couldn't look away.

# Chapter 6

# Waking on the Other Side of the World

The moment we stepped onto the airplane in Washington, D.C., there was no turning back. This was no holiday. We were leaving behind everything familiar—routine, rhythm, and all that made life predictable.

The night air was freezing, the kind of cold that makes your breath hang in the air. Wrapped in thick winter coats, MacKenzie clutched her backpack tightly, her fingers gripping the straps as if letting go would make her disappear. Pris adjusted her scarf, trying to block the chill, but nothing could stop the feeling creeping into our bones—this was real. This was happening.

Jasper, our two-year-old Schnoodle—half poodle, half schnauzer—had already been packed away in his crate, checked in like luggage. The thought of him being alone in the cargo gnawed at me, but there wasn't anything we could do. This was the only way.

Frankfurt was just transit. As we queued up for the Hyderabad flight—or at least, tried to—there was no real queue—just a flowing crowd, inching forward with practiced rhythm. The entire flight was packed with Indian families. A chaotic hum of Telugu, Hindi, and English filled the air. This wasn't a flight of suits and laptops. It was families returning to their homes, carrying stories, gifts, and dreams.

The second flight felt never-ending. Jasper was still in cargo. My mind kept calculating—he had been locked in that crate for over thirty hours now. I forced the thought away. It refused to leave.

Finally, after what felt like an eternity, the captain announced our descent into Hyderabad. I peered out of the small airplane window. Below us, a blanket of lights stretched endlessly across the land, flickering like stars trapped on the ground. The sky was dark. The city refused to sleep.

## Landing in Hyderabad: The Old Begumpet Airport

The moment the airplane door opened, a thick wave of humid air hit us. It was heavy, suffocating, inescapable.

And then, there was the smell.

Spiced. Earthy. A mix of diesel, *agarbatti*, and something I couldn't name—a scent soaked into the city's skin. It clung to us immediately, sticking to our skin, our clothes, our breath.

Even at 4 a.m., Begumpet Airport was alive. This was a place worn with time and history. The floor was scuffed, the walls dull and yellowed from age. The ceiling fans spun lazily, barely moving the thick air. The airport felt archaic—aged by time, but still standing with pride.

Baggage handlers shouted in Telugu, pushing carts stacked high with luggage. An auto-rickshaw honked from somewhere outside. A street dog wandered across the tarmac, slipping through workers' legs like it owned the place.

## A Long Wait for Luggage—And for Jasper

We pushed through the crowd towards the baggage carousel, a single, old conveyor belt squeaking under the weight of oversized suitcases.

MacKenzie stood stiffly, her arms locked around her backpack, her expression frozen. She wasn't talking. She wasn't complaining. She was just waiting, hoping it would be over soon.

Pris sighed, shifting from foot to foot. Our winter clothes were suddenly unbearable, the heat suffocating. The sweat clung to our skin, our energy draining with each passing minute.

And then, my stomach clenched.

Jasper. I checked my watch. What if something had gone wrong? What if he had been left behind? What if—

Then, finally, I saw it. His crate slid onto the conveyor belt, scuffed and filthy from the journey. Jasper was inside—wide-eyed and trembling.

MacKenzie let out a sharp breath—half relief, half desperation.

"Jasper!" she gasped, rushing forward.

The second we unlatched the door, he burst out, paws skidding against the smooth airport tiles. His entire body shook with excitement, his tail wagging furiously as he jumped onto MacKenzie, covering her in frantic licks.

It didn't matter that he had been locked away for hours. He was okay. He had found us again.

For the first time since landing, MacKenzie smiled.

## A Grand Welcome

As we stepped towards the exit, two men in crisp white shirts waited, holding fresh flower garlands. Representatives from Satyam—the company that had brought us here.

"Sir, welcome to Hyderabad," one of them said, placing a garland over Pris, MacKenzie, and me. "We have arranged a car for you. Your luggage will follow in another vehicle."

We were welcomed with such generosity. The warmth we received was humbling—and in moments, I wondered what others saw when they looked at us: opportunity, hope, or something else entirely.

I nodded, absorbing everything around me. MacKenzie did not move.

She clung to Pris, her face tight with exhaustion, her eyes filled with something I couldn't really name—fear? Disbelief? Regret?

And then, in the quietest voice, barely above a whisper, she said,

"We made a mistake. We need to go back."

We stepped outside, and Hyderabad surrounded us with sound and motion.

The streets buzzed with sputtering auto-rickshaws, the occasional ringing of a cycle bell, the distant call of a street vendor selling chai. The scent of burning incense, roasting peanuts, and damp earth filled the air.

We climbed into the car, grateful for the blast of air-conditioning. Even that couldn't suppress the weight pressing down on me.

Had we really done this?

As the car pulled away from the airport, the city unfolded before us—lights flickering, old colonial buildings standing beside towering new high-rises, the streets alive with people who belonged here.

I glanced at Pris. Then at MacKenzie, who sat silently in the back seat, clutching Jasper like a lifeline.

She stared out of the window, silent. Not speaking. Not blinking.

That night, she cried—her head buried in her mother's lap, her body shaking with the weight of emotions too heavy for words.

"Please," she whispered between sobs. "Please take me back."

We sat there, helpless, her pain filling the room like a shadow we could not escape.

We had brought her here, believing in an adventure. At that moment, all she wanted was to go home.

I knew exactly how she felt.

Because for a long time after that night, I would wake up in the middle of the night—heart pounding, convinced it had all been a dream.

That we hadn't really left home.

That we weren't really here.

But we were.

And there was no turning back.

## A New Day

When we arrived in India, we were not searching for a grand mission. We had come to work for Satyam, to build a global leadership school. Before going further, let me acknowledge the obvious. The Satyam scandal shook the corporate world, sending shockwaves through the industry and deeply affecting those of us who had invested ourselves in its vision. It was a defining moment—one that tested resilience at every level.

But this is not that story.

Of course, it impacted us. It changed the course of our journey in many ways. But what unfolded beyond that—the relationships we built, the lives that intertwined with ours, and the profound lessons in resilience and kindness—became a far greater story than any corporate downfall.

This is about that story.

## Settling In: Finding Our Place

After the press conference, we returned to the hotel, exhaustion finally catching up with us. The weight of the past few days— the long flights, the overwhelming arrival, the realisation that this wasn't a business trip but the beginning of an entirely new life—settled into my bones.

That afternoon, we met the team from Satyam—the people who would help us navigate this new world. They had arranged for a car and driver, something we quickly realised wasn't a luxury. It was a necessity. Hyderabad's traffic was unlike anything we had ever experienced—chaotic, fast-moving, yet somehow functioning in perfect rhythm.

Lanes were more of a suggestion than a rule. Motorbikes moved between cars, some carrying whole families. Auto-rickshaws made zigzag movements unpredictably. A cow stood in the middle of the road, unbothered.

The honking, the weaving of scooters, the unpredictability—it all felt too familiar. Not just because of the city, but because that's what my mind had always done too—darted, panicked, barely held together under pressure.

This wasn't just traffic. It was an ecosystem of its own.

And inside me, another kind of traffic jam had begun.

My chest tightened. My thoughts accelerated. Old anxieties—ones I thought I had left behind—began weaving their way back in, honking for attention.

We drove through the city, getting our first real glimpse of Hyderabad beyond the airport and the hotel. But I was also getting a closer look at myself—and I wasn't sure I liked what I saw.

It was a city of contrasts—gleaming high-rises and modern office complexes standing alongside centuries-old monuments and sprawling street markets. We explored residential areas, searching for a place to call home.

As I lay awake that night, I kept asking myself a question I couldn't say aloud: Had we made a mistake? Had I dragged my family across the world chasing growth while still outrunning my past?

Pris and I threw ourselves into work.

I took on the role of Chief People Officer, leading the company's talent strategy and leadership initiatives, while Pris became Head of Executive Development and Coaching, working closely with Satyam's top executives to refine their skills and elevate their impact.

She didn't just lead coaching sessions—she built trust that ran deep. Her calm, steady presence drew people in, especially women on the team. She wasn't seen as just a leader. She was a guide—wise, grounded, and direct.

One of her team members came into work one scorching summer day wearing a black turtleneck. That alone was enough for Pris to pause. She didn't wait for signs. She didn't sidestep it. She already had the trust.

She looked her in the eye and said, "I know something isn't right. And you don't have to keep living this way."

It wasn't a soft conversation. It was a lifeline.

The woman broke down. She had been suffering in silence—afraid, unsure. Pris helped her see that she didn't need anyone's permission to leave—she needed her own. With her support, she made the decision to walk away from the abuse.

That choice saved her life.

Today, that woman lives in the United States. She is thriving, independent, and still close to our family. We see her often—and each time, we're reminded of the force Pris is—the kind of leader who sees what others miss, and acts when others hesitate.

## Moving into Our New Home

In early January, we moved into a newly constructed colony of homes, a small gated community with small gardens—a rarity in a city where space was a luxury.

As we unpacked our belongings, arranging the furniture, hanging up photos and art, I found myself staring out of the window.

And I wondered:

Would this ever feel like home? Or would we always be caught between two worlds?

# Expectations vs. Reality: Our First Lesson in India

When the offer came to work for Satyam, we decided to move to India without ever visiting first. Even though they offered us a pre-move trip, we declined. We knew jet lag would leave us too exhausted, and more than likely, we would overthink everything and talk ourselves out of it. Instead, we asked them to send us a video of potential neighbourhoods, so we could get a sense of what life might be like.

What they sent us was beautiful.

The video played with soaring music, slow-motion shots of lush green spaces, tree-lined walking paths, and grand homes with manicured gardens. They even toured a house for us, saying, "This is the kind of place you will be living in."

It was stunning. It reassured us that we were making the right choice, that we were about to embark on an exciting new adventure, with a level of comfort we had not expected.

Then, we arrived in India.

When the realtor began showing us homes, something felt off. Instead of sprawling estates and lush greenery, we were being shown cramped neighbourhoods, tiny gardens, and houses that felt musty and dark.

Confused, I finally asked, "Where is the neighbourhood from the video? That is where we want to live."

The realtor gave me a puzzled look.

"Show me the video," he said.

I pulled out my laptop, inserted the CD they had sent us, and let it play.

The moment the video began, the realtor laughed.

Pris and I exchanged looks. Taken aback, I asked, "What is so funny?"

He shook his head, still chuckling.

"This is not a neighbourhood," he said. "That is a public park in town."

My stomach sank.

"And the home?" I asked slowly, already dreading the answer.

He grinned. "That is the home of Ramalinga Raju—your CEO."

We felt completely deceived.

It took time to move past the disappointment and frustration.

Ultimately, we were not deterred. We kept searching. And eventually, we did find a place that we could call home for the next several years.

## MacKenzie's Transition

The transition to India wasn't easy for any of us, but it was especially hard on MacKenzie. At fifteen, the change felt overwhelming. The constant noise—the relentless honking, buzzing scooters, the calls of street vendors—seemed to echo without pause. Packs of stray dogs barked and howled through the night, sometimes in pain. What upset her most wasn't just the noise, but the way people treated the street dogs. Stones thrown. Brooms swung. Or worse—complete indifference.

One day, while travelling with Pris along a crowded main road, they saw a teenage boy weaving through traffic on a two-wheeler without a helmet. Just seconds later, he was hit.

The sound of the impact, the screeching tyres, the stillness that followed—he didn't survive. The ride home was silent. MacKenzie couldn't speak. Neither could Pris.

All of it—the chaos, the cruelty, the unfamiliarity—left MacKenzie disoriented and longing for what she had left behind. One evening, after yet another day of holding it together, she sat us down and said, "I've given it a chance. I really have. But I want to go back home." She asked if we could send her back to America—to enrol her in boarding school and let her finish her studies there. It wasn't a meltdown or dramatic plea. It was a sincere ask from a young girl trying to find her place in a world that felt nothing like her own.

Pris, ever calm and grounded, gently placed her hand on MacKenzie's arm and said, "It's alright to feel like this. You don't have to love it right away. Just give it a bit more time."

MacKenzie shook her head. "I already have."

And yet … something shifted.

She made a friend. Then another. She picked up bits of Telugu and slowly began to find her rhythm in this new world. Kavitha, our housekeeper, invited her into the kitchen, where MacKenzie learned how to make rasam and potato fry, and eventually even mastered the art of *tadka*. She taught her classmates how to make peanut butter and jelly sandwiches— something they'd never seen before. She still missed home, of course, but her laughter slowly returned. So did her curiosity.

As for me, I was adjusting too—but there were moments that caught me completely off guard. One night, I was startled awake by a loud, piercing whistle from somewhere outside. Then again—another whistle. And another. It kept happening, almost every hour. The next morning, I asked a neighbour about it. They explained it was the night watchman walking through the colony, blowing his whistle to stay awake and signal his presence. Apparently, this was common practice—meant to assure residents he was on patrol and to prevent him from dozing off. While I understood the logic, it was maddening. It made it nearly impossible to sleep. Eventually, I figured out that if I kept the A/C on high, the noise would drown out the whistle and allow me to rest.

## Beyond the Walls

Weeks later, feeling the need to explore beyond our compound, Pris and I decided to step out. We greeted the guards at the gate with a warm "Namaskaaram" and headed up the hill. Just a short walk away, we came upon a large cluster of tents where hundreds of families lived. They were in the midst of celebrating Sankranti—the harvest festival. As we approached, smiling and waving, they motioned for us to join in. Everyone was dancing, laughing, and enjoying the celebrations. Though we were strangers, they welcomed us with open arms and offered us food, which we gratefully accepted.

Then, one of the adults whispered something in Telugu to a young boy and handed him a few rupees. Off he went. When he returned, he was holding two ice-cold Diet Cokes, which the women smilingly placed in our hands. They didn't speak much English. We didn't speak much Telugu—just a few words like *dhanyavaadalu* (thank you). And yet, none of that mattered. There was laughter, warmth, and joy. And it needed no translation.

We danced. We smiled. We belonged, if only for a moment. And in that moment, it became profoundly clear: no matter how little they had in material terms, they had each other. That spontaneous act of generosity shifted something in us. It reshaped our understanding of what it means to have "enough."

As we began settling into this new life, we had no idea that someone else had been watching us closely—not someone from the corporate world or media, but by someone much closer.

# Chapter 7

# Meeting the Foreigners

For the next few days, I continued to watch them from a distance.

They had a driver—Hyderabad's traffic was chaotic, even for us, so I understood why they wouldn't dare drive themselves.

But something about the way they moved, the way they belonged to a different rhythm of life—it pulled at something I couldn't name.

I kept watching. Day after day.

These people told me something—this girl, this family—weren't just passing through. I didn't know it yet, but my world was about to tilt in a way I never expected.

The girl lingered outside each morning, walking her little white dog. She took slow, hesitant steps, as if she didn't quite know where she was supposed to be. Most newcomers stared at everything—eyes wide, hungry to soak in the strangeness of this place.

She looked lost, as if searching for someone she'd left behind.

Amma noticed her too, standing on the doorway with her arms crossed, observing with interest. Jyothi, always full of questions, watched closely from the veranda, her dark eyes tracking every movement.

"She looks sad," she murmured. "Like she doesn't want to be here."

I nodded, but said nothing. There was a heaviness in the girl's shoulders that reminded me of the mornings when I didn't want to go school either—her sadness felt different— like a weight she didn't know how to put down.

Each morning, after walking her dog, she crouched down, gave it a quick pat on the head, then disappeared through the gate. Moments later, the yellow school bus would arrive. She dragged herself toward it, her backpack hung loose, her steps dragging like they had no energy left.

The other kids chattered and laughed, but she never joined them. She always sat by the window, earphones in, gaze locked on the streets like she was trying to disappear into them.

And then—after she had gone—something even stranger happened.

The front door of their house would swing open again. The man and woman rushed out, moving fast, their voices clipped as they exchanged hurried words. The driver stood waiting, holding the car door.

And the little white dog?

It trotted out after them, tail wagging, hopping into the car like it had a job to do. Not once, not twice—every single day.

It perched by the window, ears perked, eyes alert—like it had its own important places to be.

I didn't understand their world. I wasn't even sure they understood each other. But I couldn't stop watching.

Maybe because some part of me—quiet and still—was wondering what it would feel like to be the girl.

Jyothi gasped. "Amma! Look!" she pointed, eyes widening with disbelief.

Amma shook her head, a small smile tugging at the corner of her mouth. "Ayyoo," she muttered, watching the car pull away. "Even the dogs here have drivers."

Jyothi giggled. "Maybe it goes to work," she said, half-joking, half-serious. "Maybe it's secretly the boss of something."

We didn't know where it went, or why. It made us wonder.

Still, it wasn't the dog that kept my attention—it was the girl.

She didn't want to be here. I could see that.

And then, one evening, everything changed.

I had been watching them again, unsure whether I should get closer. They weren't like the other families in the colony—there was something different about them. They felt like a puzzle piece that didn't fit, like an answer to a question I hadn't asked yet.

Then, just as I turned back to my books, I sensed movement.

I looked up.

She was standing right in front of me.

## Our First Meeting

"Hey," she said.

I froze.

Up close, she looked even more out of place. Her jeans were slightly ripped at the knees, her T-shirt loose and casual—not at all like the pressed uniforms the girls at my school wore.

"I'm MacKenzie," she said, rocking back on her heels. "What's your name?"

No one had ever just walked up to me like that before. Especially not someone like her.

"Devi," I said.

Her eyes flicked to my books. "Are you studying?"

I nodded.

"For school?"

Another nod.

She smiled, then—an easy, natural smile—and plopped down beside me on the dusty pavement, completely unbothered by the dirt.

"What's your favourite subject?" she asked.

I hesitated. Amma never asked what I liked. Amma only cared that I studied, that I kept my promise.

"Maths," I said, uncertain.

"Ugh," MacKenzie groaned, tilting her head back. "I hate math."

I couldn't help it. A small laugh escaped me.

Her grin widened, pleased.

Then, before I could react, the soft and warm dog landed in my lap.

"Jasper!" she called, but the tiny dog had already settled, paws pressing against my book, tongue darting out to lick my fingers.

I stiffened.

Street dogs didn't do this.

They kept their distance, their wariness etched into them by years of hunger and struggle. This little dog wasn't afraid. He wasn't cautious. He was simply … happy.

"Sorry," MacKenzie said, reaching for him, but I shook my head.

Slowly, hesitantly, I ran my fingers through his fur. It was softer than I imagined. Like nothing I had ever felt before.

I giggled—softly, uncertainly—but it was real.

MacKenzie leaned back, resting her chin on her hand. "You know," she said, "we just moved here from Virginia, and I don't really know anyone here yet. Maybe you could show me around sometime?"

I stared at her and wondered. Me? Show her around?

"Where is Virginia?" Devi asked, tilting her head.

MacKenzie blinked. "It's in America."

Devi had heard of America, of course—everyone had. It was on TV and in the movies. People talked about it like it was a dream, a place full of opportunities, towering buildings, and streets so clean they shone under the sunlight.

"America ..." Devi repeated, her voice tinged with something between curiosity and longing. "I never met anyone from America before."

MacKenzie gave a small shrug. "I guess. I liked Virginia because it was quiet. Lots of trees, big open spaces."

"I ... I don't know much," I admitted, still trying to understand why she was even talking to me.

"Well," MacKenzie said with a grin, "then we can learn together. What do you say?"

I hesitated—but nodded.

## A Seat at Their Table

About a week later, she invited me inside their home.

"Come over," MacKenzie said casually, like it was the simplest thing in the world.

Inside?

I had never been invited inside before—certainly not into a house like hers.

She nodded toward the open door. "Yeah! My parents won't mind."

Her confidence felt like an open door.

My feet refused to move. I tightened my grip on the edge of my dupatta, the fabric crumpling in my hands.

Stepping inside meant stepping into a world that wasn't mine.

A world that felt too polished. Too effortless.

What if I did something wrong? What if they changed their minds and realised I didn't belong?

I turned slightly, searching for Amma. She was sweeping near our doorway, her movements slow, deliberate.

Our eyes met.

For a moment, she didn't say anything—just studied me, her gaze unreadable. Was she worried? Proud? Afraid I might not come back the same?

Then, ever so slightly, she nodded.

A silent permission.

I paused at the edge of the doorway. Everything inside looked so different—clean, gentle in a way I hadn't expected.

I wasn't sure where to step, or how to carry myself in a world like that.

Not because I didn't belong—but because I had never learned the language of comfort.

What if I said the wrong thing? What if I stood in the wrong place?

I swallowed hard and stepped forward.

Inside was unlike anything I had ever seen.

The air smelled sweet and unfamiliar, a mix of vanilla and something warm—like cinnamon or cardamom, but softer.

The floor was cool beneath my bare feet, smooth like polished stone.

Light streamed through enormous windows, making everything feel impossibly open.

Their home had the same layout as Raji Madam's family's house—just furnished differently. They had American-style furniture instead of Indian, with new Indian rugs stretched across the floors like they had always belonged.

The furniture was plush, like something from a movie set—too perfect to be real.

At the dining table, a man with sharp features sat behind an open laptop. His eyes flicked toward me—assessing, but not unkind.

He gave a little smile.

"Hello," he said in slow, clear English.

No one like him had ever spoken to me before—a foreigner in formal clothes, living in a world far from mine.

I nodded quickly, unsure if I was supposed to respond.

Before I could decide, a woman appeared from the kitchen, with short reddish-blonde hair. She carried a tray with glasses of juice.

"You must be Devi," she said warmly. "MacKenzie has told us about you."

I swallowed. She has?

"Yes," I murmured.

MacKenzie flopped onto the couch, stretching out like she had lived there forever. "She's really smart," she declared. "She studies all the time."

The woman smiled. "Oh? What do you want to be when you grow up, Devi?"

I tried to speak—but nothing came out.

People asked when I would marry. When I would work. Never what I dreamed of becoming.

Never what I wanted.

"I don't know—I … I want to study," I said finally, my voice smaller than I intended.

The woman glanced at the man, and something passed between them—something silent, something I didn't understand.

Not yet.

MacKenzie patted the seat beside her. "Come sit."

## More Than Just a Meal

"Why don't you stay for dinner, Devi?" the woman asked.

I stood there, unsure what to say. No one had ever invited me like that before.

I looked down and mumbled, "No … I should go."

She didn't push. She simply smiled and waited, her tone gentle, like she truly meant it.

After a moment, I said softly, "I have to ask my mother."

She nodded. "Of course."

I stepped outside and hurried home. My mother was in the kitchen, folding clothes, her hands moving without pause. I asked her in a low voice if I could stay for dinner at the foreigner's house.

She looked at me with surprise. Then, after a pause, she said, "Okay. But don't be late."

I ran back, breathless, trying not to seem too eager.

"I can stay," I said when the woman opened the door.

Her eyes brightened. "Good. Come in, Devi."

The dining table gleamed under the soft yellow light.

At home, we sat on the floor, knees tucked in, plates on our laps. We didn't speak. We just ate—quickly, without waste.

But here, everything was different.

People talked. They smiled. They passed bowls to one another. They waited until everyone had food before starting to eat. Even the way they held their forks and knives looked graceful to me.

I sat at their table. The man smiled at me kindly. The girl—MacKenzie—chatted like we had known each other for years.

They didn't treat me like an outsider. No one looked at me strangely.

That night, I didn't just eat food.

I tasted something else—kindness.

And for the first time in my life, I felt what it might be like to belong.

# Chapter 8

# A Place That Feels Like Family

From then on, their home became familiar to me. The more time I spent there, the less I felt like an outsider. It was no longer just a house I visited—it became a place where I felt welcomed, where no one questioned why I was there.

One day, the woman gently said, "You can call me Aunty."

The man added with a warm smile, "And me—Uncle."

I was taken aback. No one outside my family had ever said that to me before.

Just those two words—Uncle and Aunty—meant more than they could imagine. Something shifted inside me. It wasn't just kindness—they were including me, as if I was part of them.

They asked me about school, about my dreams—things I had rarely spoken of, even at home.

Ed Uncle would proudly introduce me to his friends, calling me bright, telling them I was full of potential. He spoke to me like I had something worth saying, like my voice mattered.

Aunty listened with the same gentle warmth. Her eyes were always kind, her words full of encouragement. She asked me about my studies, my favourite books, even those silly memories from school I usually kept to myself. She asked real questions—the kind that made me feel seen.

And MacKenzie—she never treated me like I was different. With her, I wasn't just the girl from the neighbouring lane. I was her friend. Her equal.

I often brought my little cousin brother, Raja, along with me. He was four-years-old—shy, wide-eyed, always clinging to my hand whenever we went somewhere new. But here, in this home, he didn't hesitate. They welcomed him just as they had welcomed me—not as an extra mouth to feed, but as if he truly belonged.

Raja had been living with us since he was just two years and seven months old. His mother, my aunt, had two sons. They believed at least one of them should have the chance to study in the city. So, they sent Raja to stay with us.

He had grown up with me, like my own little brother. I felt responsible for him—his safety, his learning, his happiness.

In this house, I didn't have to explain who he was or protect him. They simply accepted him.

They asked him if he wanted more food before he had even finished his plate. They smiled at him the way family does—genuinely, with softness in their eyes. They even let him hold Jasper, their tiny dog, though he had never touched a pet before. He had always been afraid of animals, but here, he wasn't.

It was such a small thing, but to me, it meant the world.

They didn't treat him like the maid's nephew. They didn't treat me like the househelp's daughter.

We sat together at the dining table, eating fresh meals and passing dishes like it was the most natural thing in the world. The food was simple, but somehow it felt special—grilled chicken, warm vegetables, rice on some days, fruit after dinner. It wasn't like the grand wedding feasts where the plates overflowed. This was different. Everything was thoughtfully prepared, carefully placed, and always served with care.

At home, Amma cooked quickly, serving straight from the pot. "Eat fast," she would say, needing to return to work. There was no time to sit together. No waiting. Just eat and move on.

But here, no one started until everyone had food. They passed bowls around. They checked if I wanted more. They made sure Raj had something he liked.

When they served me, it wasn't rushed. It wasn't about filling a plate. It felt like they were serving a person—like I mattered.

I sat on the same sofa as MacKenzie, watching shows I'd never seen before, laughing without thinking. There was no separate corner for me, no feeling of being watched, no sense that I should leave soon.

Over time, they became more than neighbours. They became something close to family.

And as the days passed, I became so comfortable in their home that sometimes, they even invited me to stay overnight.

MacKenzie treated me like a sister. She didn't have to. But she chose to—every single time. She shared her things, laughed with me, and asked for my opinions. She never acted like she was doing me a favour.

Of course, I noticed everything—what they had, what I didn't. But I didn't let that bother me. I didn't want charity. I wanted an opportunity. And I was determined to prove that

I belonged, not because of their kindness—but because I had something worthy in me.

For the first time, I wasn't trying to hide my background. I wasn't ashamed of where I came from. But I also knew—I was capable of something more.

And somehow, they saw it too.

## Sweet 16 for MacKenzie

That summer, as MacKenzie's sixteenth birthday approached, she invited Raja and me to the grand party her parents were hosting at a fancy restaurant.

I had never been to a party like that before. The thought of all the people, the music, the lights—it felt like something from a film, a world far from my own. Still, the invitation made me feel special, like I was being included in something important.

Then reality settled in.

We had no extra money for clothes, and I couldn't ask Amma. She worked too hard already and buying new clothes just for a party felt like a luxury we couldn't afford. The idea of adding another burden, even a small one, made my stomach twist.

When MacKenzie asked if I was coming, I hesitated. "I'm not sure," I said softly. "I need to ask my mother."

She frowned slightly but nodded. "I get it. Let me know."

I smiled in return, but inside, I already knew the answer. The problem wasn't permission—it was what I didn't have.

Later, MacKenzie must have spoken to Ed Uncle, because the next day, when I arrived at their house, he greeted me with a warm smile. "Devi, I need to go shopping. Would you and Raja like to come along?"

I paused, unsure. I wasn't used to gifts or being given things for no reason. "I have to ask my mother first."

After getting Amma's approval, we piled into the car. John, their driver, greeted me with his usual kind smile as he held the door open.

Beside me, Ed Uncle adjusted his glasses and glanced back. "Ready for an adventure, Devi?"

I nodded, though I wasn't sure what to expect.

From the beginning, Ed Uncle had been different from anyone I had known. He carried himself with confidence, yet he never made me feel small. His kindness wasn't loud or obvious—it was in the little things. The way he asked about my studies, how he listened when I spoke, how he noticed things most people overlooked.

Like today.

He must have sensed my hesitation about the party, and understood the unspoken worry in my silence. Because without making a big deal out of it, without making it feel like charity, he had simply created a way for me to be part of it.

As John navigated the crowded Hyderabad streets, I stole a glance at Ed Uncle. He was scrolling through his phone, occasionally looking up to point out something interesting— an old movie poster peeling off a wall, a street vendor carrying an impossible number of baskets on his head.

"See that?" he said, nudging MacKenzie. "Now that's talent."

She rolled her eyes. "Dad, you say that every time."

"And I mean it every time," he replied with a grin.

His ease, his warmth—it made things feel simpler.

When we arrived at the store, I hesitated for just a moment before stepping out of the car. The building was huge, its glass doors reflecting the bright lights inside. I had never been anywhere like this before.

Sensing my hesitation, Ed Uncle gave a small nod. "Come on, Devi. Let's find you something special."

And in that moment, I knew—this wasn't just about a dress.

It was about making sure I never felt like I didn't belong.

The salespeople, dressed neatly in uniforms, spoke in soft, polite voices, treating us as though we belonged there.

I wasn't sure I did.

I had never been on an escalator before.

I stood at the edge, watching the moving steps glide up and disappear. My heart pounded. It was as if the ground itself was shifting, and I wasn't sure I could trust it.

"Just step on," MacKenzie said, grinning. "It'll do the work for you."

I swallowed hard. That was what scared me—the idea of something carrying me forward without my control.

I hesitated, gripping the railing tightly, my knuckles turning white. Finally, I forced myself forward, stepping onto the metal step just as it lifted. My stomach lurched, my body tensed, adjusting to the strange sensation of being moved without walking.

MacKenzie laughed—not in a mean way—like she was watching something innocent, something new. She thought it was funny, but she didn't make me feel small.

"See? Not so bad."

I nodded, though my legs still felt shaky.

When we reached the top, I stepped off too quickly, nearly stumbling. John, who had been watching, gave me a knowing smile. "It happens to everyone for the first time."

I exhaled, relieved.

And then, as I turned, my breath caught.

The young ladies' section stretched before me in rows of colours and textures. Silk, chiffon, embroidered designs—clothing I had only seen in magazines or on women passing by in places I didn't belong.

I wandered through the aisles in a daze. Everything looked beautiful, delicate, and expensive.

I didn't belong here.

Ed Uncle must have noticed the hesitation in my steps because he turned to me with a gentle smile. "Let's find something for the party."

I froze, my fingers instinctively tightening around my dupatta.

For me?

I had never picked out something new before. My clothes had always been passed down, stitched, or borrowed.

Sensing my discomfort, Ed Uncle didn't push. He simply walked beside me, as if this was the most natural thing in the world.

MacKenzie, on the other hand, dove right in.

"This one!" she said excitedly, holding up a soft pink dress with lace sleeves.

I barely had time to shake my head before she grabbed another—deep blue, covered in tiny embroidered flowers. "Or this! Oh wait, this one would look amazing on you!"

I couldn't help but smile at her enthusiasm.

Together, they guided me through the racks, helping me pick something elegant yet simple. Something that felt like me.

Not just for me—Raja, too.

I watched as Ed Uncle carefully picked out crisp shirts and well-fitted trousers for my little brother, making sure the colours suited him. When Raja tried them on, he stood a little taller, his small frame suddenly looking more grown-up.

I had never seen him look so confident.

And that was when it hit me.

It wasn't about the clothes.

It was about what they were doing.

They saw me. They saw Raja.

They wanted us to be included.

I stepped into the fitting room, my hands trembling slightly as I pulled the dress over my head.

The fabric was softer than anything I had ever worn. It flowed around me like water, the intricate designs catching the light as I turned to the mirror.

I barely recognized the girl in the mirror—she looked ... sure of herself. Even if just a little.

For a brief moment, I let myself imagine—what if?

What if I could be part of this world?

What if I wasn't just Devi from the servant's quarters?

Then, just as quickly, doubt crept in.

No matter what I wore, I was still me. Still the girl who came from small, cramped rooms. Still the girl whose mother scrubbed floors, so others could live in houses like this.

I wasn't like them.

I would never be like them.

## A Night to Remember

The night of the party arrived, and as we stepped into the restaurant, it felt like entering another world.

Soft golden lights sparkled the room, making everything glow. The tables gleamed under the twinkling chandeliers, and the air was filled with laughter, voices blending into a soft, happy hum. The scent of rich spices, freshly baked bread, and something sweet drifted around me, making my stomach tighten—not just with hunger, but with anticipation.

Music pulsed through the space, the deep bass vibrating through the floor. The lights flashed in rhythm, making the whole room feel alive.

I felt small, like a visitor in a world that wasn't mine.

Then MacKenzie spotted me.

Her face lit up, her eyes sparkling. "You look amazing, Devi!" she said, her voice warm, full of something I couldn't quite name. Pride? Joy?

Something inside me softened.

I looked around, still overwhelmed. The guests were dressed in dazzling outfits, moving effortlessly, talking, laughing. No one seemed out of place. No one seemed to notice how different Raja and I were from everyone present there.

I glanced at him—his face mirrored my own awe. We had stepped into a different reality, one where, for the first time, we weren't outsiders.

The music wrapped around us, filling my chest with its steady beat. I smiled, just a little. No one was staring. No one was whispering.

MacKenzie introduced me to everyone, weaving me into the crowd as if I had always belonged.

And then, for the first time, I danced.

At first, I was stiff, unsure. My feet felt heavy, my hands awkward. MacKenzie laughed, spinning me until I couldn't help but move. The lights, the music, the energy—it was exhilarating.

Even Raja, usually so quiet, let loose, his small feet bouncing to the beat.

For the first time, I wasn't thinking about where I had come from. I wasn't weighed down by what I didn't have.

For once, I wasn't overthinking. I was just dancing.

But then, something else caught my eye—the food.

A buffet stretched before us, rows of shining silver trays filled with dishes more extravagant than anything I had ever imagined.

Spice-scented biryani, steaming hot. Golden *naan* stacked high. Creamy dal, rich with ghee. Crisp salads with bright red tomatoes and drizzles of a dressing I had never tasted before.

And the desserts.

*Gulab jamun*—warm and syrupy. Jalebis—bright orange and glistening. Kheer—rich and creamy, topped with leaves of saffron.

I hesitated. Should I take some? Was it okay? Did I deserve to be here, eating like this?

MacKenzie grinned, nudging me forward. "Come on, you have to try this!"

Tentatively, I reached for a plate. The first bite exploded with flavours—spicy, sweet, creamy, and rich, all at once. My senses became alive.

Even Raja, usually so reserved, couldn't stop eating, his eyes wide with delight.

I couldn't remember the last time I had eaten like this.

But as the night wore on, something stirred inside me. I was enjoying the food, the music, the laughter—but somewhere deep down, I knew this wasn't my world. Not really. Not yet.

This was my glimpse into another world—a world that still felt just out of reach.

I was part of it for the moment, yes. But I didn't know if I belonged, if this would continue. Was it all just a fleeting dream?

# Chapter 9

# Meeting the Girl Next Door

We left behind the chilled, chai-scented boardrooms of HITEC City and entered the evening's familiar chaos—autos honking, bikes darting like dragonflies, buses groaning around tight corners.

We passed Durgam Cheruvu on the left, its waters catching the last light, flanked by coaching centre hoardings and half-finished buildings. Jubilee Hills Check Post came next, where the city changed tone—less buildings, more trees. Fruit stalls. Big gates. A temple bell rang in the distance—sharp, solitary, followed by a crow's call and the shriek of a pressure cooker.

By the time we turned into Film Nagar, the sun had dipped. The lanes narrowed, cows rested under, "No Parking" signs, and a schoolboy zipped past on a cycle. A curve. A slope.

Road No. 13. Almost home.

It was still hot. That kind of sticky, end-of-the-day heat that clings to your clothing and seeps into your bones, even after the sun has gone soft behind the rooftops.

By the time we reached our gate, we were both done— emotionally, physically, mentally. The city welcomed us with open arms—and unfiltered energy. Noise and dust pressed in from every side—yet beneath it all, a strange rhythm pulsed, welcoming and wild. And we were still learning how to breathe in its rhythm.

John slowed the car at the gate, stepped out, and pulled it open with practised ease. The hinges gave their familiar groan as the gate swung wide. Tyres rolled over sun-baked granite—typical of Hyderabad compounds.

Pris sat beside me. Her eyes were fixed on the window, her expression unreadable. We hadn't said much on the drive back. There are silences that feel empty, and then there are the ones that carry too much. This was the latter.

Jasper, curled up in the backseat, stirred as we came to a halt near the front veranda. He let out a low whine, then tapped his tail gently against the seat. Even he seemed drained.

I inhaled slowly, as though drawing strength from the heavy, dust-laced air. John closed the gate behind us with a familiar clang. The scent of biryani—or maybe *pulihora* mixed with homemade *avakai*—floated in, familiar and mouthwatering. I couldn't say for sure, but it stirred something achingly familiar.

"We're home," I said. But as I looked toward the girl bent over her notebook, I wondered—whose home was it really becoming?

Pris nodded, but didn't move.

I stepped out first, stretching as I did. The stiffness in my neck reminded me just how long I'd been upright. Jasper leapt out behind me, tail wagging, nose to the ground, already investigating every scent like he was mapping the territory.

I turned to help Pris out, but she was already opening her door. She stepped out slowly, adjusting her business suit with one hand and shielding her eyes from the porch light with the other. She was trying—more than I could ever say out loud.

And that's when I saw her.

## The Girl Beyond the Wall

Just beyond the wall.

A flicker of movement. Small. Still.

I turned my head toward the far end of the compound, to the neighbour's side. A low cement wall separated the properties. Nothing grand. Just the usual kind—paint flaking a little, moss at the base. Enough to divide one world from another.

And there, under the soft buzz of a single bulb hanging outside the back doorway, sat a girl.

Cross-legged. Silent. Still.

Her pencil scratched the page like it was her only weapon against the world. That fragile notebook—creased, smudged—held her entire future between its worn pages. She couldn't have been more than twelve or thirteen. Thin. Barefoot. Her school uniform hung loosely on her small frame, the collar slipping off one shoulder. A long braided plait ran down her back, already starting to come undone.

She didn't notice me.

Her pencil moved across the page in short, careful strokes. Her lips moved too—silently, rhythmically—as if repeating the lines to herself. Maybe grammar rules. Maybe science. Maybe spelling. It didn't matter.

Every so often she paused, frowned, erased something, and began again.

Around her, the city was humming in the evening— pressure cookers whistling, children laughing in the background, someone arguing on the phone, a scooter sputtering up the road—but none of it touched her.

She was in a world of her own. Focused. Fierce.

And I stood there, watching, longer than I meant to.

Not because I was intruding.

But because I recognised that posture.

That straight-backed focus? It wasn't about marks. It came from knowing this might be her only way forward.

From the porch, Pris asked, "Everything okay?"

I didn't turn around. Just nodded. "Yeah. Just ... give me a minute."

The girl still hadn't looked up.

She had no idea I was watching.

And yet in that moment, I felt like I'd stumbled into something private. Something sacred. A glimpse into a life unfolding—purposefully—just a few feet beyond my own.

I didn't know her name.

We didn't speak that night.

She stayed in her world, and I stayed in mine—overwhelmed, unsettled, not yet ready to admit that something inside me had shifted.

But as I turned to go inside, I looked back once more over my shoulder.

She was still there. Still writing. Still holding her future in that fragile little notebook as if letting go would mean losing everything.

And somehow, without knowing how or why, I knew I would remember her.

Days passed.

Life settled into its strange new rhythm: honking horns at dawn, jasmine drifting through open windows, the smell of sambar wafting in from a neighbouring kitchen, power cuts at the worst possible moments, and MacKenzie collecting stories faster than I could keep up. She was adjusting quicker than any of us, finding her way in a world that still felt like a puzzle to me.

## The Moment Our Worlds Touched

And then, one afternoon, I came home to find her in our living room.

The same girl.

The same shoulders drawn tight, as if every bone in her body was bracing for the wrong word.

The first time I met Devi, she was standing just past the entryway, her small frame rigid, her dark eyes darting around as if she didn't quite belong. It was MacKenzie who had brought her over.

"Daddy, this is my friend," she said casually, as if it were the most normal thing in the world. She still called me Daddy—a small thing I silently cherished, a thread that connected us no matter how many countries we moved through.

Devi stood just behind her, clutching the edge of her dupatta with both hands, her shoulders tense. She looked like she wanted to shrink into the wall.

But I knew her. Not by name. Not by story.

I knew the way she held herself, the way her eyes scanned the room looking for an escape route. I'd seen it before—in a mirror, in a memory. And just a few nights earlier, in the quiet glow of a neighbour's porch light.

Pris stepped forward first, her warmth effortless. "It's so nice to meet you," she said, offering a kind smile.

I nodded. "Hi. I've seen you studying outside."

Devi's eyes flickered to mine, startled. Her lips parted slightly in surprise. Then the smallest nod. "Yes, Uncle," she whispered.

MacKenzie grinned. "She's really smart, Daddy. She studies all the time only."

Devi's fingers tightened around her scarf. I could tell she wasn't used to this—to being noticed like this.

Pris gestured toward the sofa. "Come, sit," she said.

Devi hesitated before perching on the edge of the cushion, as if ready to flee at any moment.

"Would you like some juice?" she asked.

She nodded shyly, whispering, "Thank you ma'am."

MacKenzie flopped down beside her, her ease in stark contrast to Devi's stiffness. "She wants to be a doctor," she announced with full confidence.

Devi's eyes widened, and she shook her head quickly. "No, no … I only want to study," she said softly.

"Same thing," MacKenzie shrugged.

I chuckled at my daughter's faith in her new friend. "That's a great goal."

For the next hour, Devi mostly listened as we chatted, her responses short and careful. There was something in her eyes—an intelligence, a hunger.

It reminded me of the boy I used to be, the one who had clung to books like they were his only way out. Who had known that education wasn't just a dream—it was the lifeline.

## Stay for Dinner

As Pris moved around the kitchen, she glanced toward Devi. "You should stay for dinner."

Devi sat up straighter, her fingers curling into her lap. "No …
I should go home," she said quickly.

"You're already here," Pris said with an easy smile. "It's
just a meal."

MacKenzie nudged her playfully. "Stay. We eat normal
food, I promise."

Devi hesitated, her gaze flickering toward the door. I could
tell she was weighing the decision, trying to decide whether it
was okay. Whether she was allowed.

Finally, she nodded. "Okay."

That night, we ate together, and I watched as the tension
in her shoulders eased just slightly. It was a small thing—one
meal—but in hindsight, I realise it was the moment everything
changed.

She took a bite, hesitated for a moment, then took
another. I saw it in her face—relief, comfort, a fleeting moment
of safety.

And suddenly, I was a boy again.

A plate shattering against the floor.

My mother's hands were trembling as she set down dinner.

My sister's eyes fixed on her lap, willing herself to
disappear.

The scrape of my father's chair, the slow, deliberate rise
of his voice.

"You call this dinner?"

The knife—red handle, gleaming blade.

Cold metal pressing against my throat.

"Are you ready to die?"

Not breathing. Not moving.

A fork clinking against a plate.

Devi glancing up, searching my face.

Her shoulders relaxed—just a little, but enough to notice.

No yelling. No breaking. Just … eating.

Pris's voice cut through the haze.

"Where did you go?"

I blinked.

"Nowhere," I murmured. We both knew that wasn't true.

## A Revelation

Over the months that followed, Devi became like one of our own. At first, she was quiet—hesitant, unsure where she truly belonged. But MacKenzie welcomed her like a younger sister, without a second thought. And Pris, with her warm heart and open arms, ensured she always felt seen and included.

Slowly, there began a shift. Devi's confidence grew—not just in herself, but in her voice. She began speaking more in English, and soon, she was helping us translate whenever workers or neighbours came to the house. Her command over language and fluency made her a bridge between our world and the one outside the gate. She didn't just translate words—she conveyed emotions, making sure nothing got lost between languages. With poise, she brought people together, one conversation at a time.

Whenever someone came to the door and we couldn't understand each other, we would simply say, "Call Devi—she will manage." And she always did.

One evening, I found her sitting at the dining table, flipping through one of MacKenzie's textbooks, her lips moving as she read silently to herself.

"You like math?" I asked, sitting down across from her.

She nodded, glancing up nervously. "Yes."

I leaned back. "I loved math. It was my favourite subject in school."

She blinked, clearly surprised. "Really?"

I laughed. "Really. Numbers—they always made more sense to me."

A small smile appeared on her lips. It was one of the first times I saw her relax.

As time passed, Devi found her rhythm with us. She wasn't just a guest—she was family. She spent time and laughed with MacKenzie. Little by little, she let her guard down. Her confidence grew, her voice steadier, her dreams bigger.

One evening, I found Devi sitting in the living room with Pris. Pris was on the sofa, a book resting in her lap. The room was quiet, but I could feel it heavy in the air—like everyone had taken a deep breath and wasn't sure how to let it out. Devi sat nearby, cross-legged on the floor, watching TV with MacKenzie.

It wasn't a conversation I meant to overhear, but I stood for a moment at the edge of the hallway, listening.

Pris looked at her and said, "You don't speak much around adults, Devi. But I see how you are with MacKenzie—confident, curious, quick-witted."

Devi glanced up, a little surprised, not quite sure what to say.

Pris didn't fill the void of silence. She simply continued, her voice even and direct. "You don't have to be small to be respectful. There's a difference between being humble and hiding. You have a presence. Don't shrink from it."

That was Pris. Steady. Discerning. She spoke rarely in moments like these, but when she did, it was with clarity that lingered.

Devi didn't respond immediately, but I saw it—the subtle shift. Her shoulders lifted, her spine straightened. It wasn't dramatic. It was quieter. Deeper.

She had heard her. And something inside her believed it.

Devi's transformation mirrored what we were noticing around us—change, in all its forms, wasn't always welcomed. As she grew more confident, and as we settled more deeply into life in Hyderabad, the ripples of our presence began reaching further than we realised. Not everyone saw us through the same lens we saw them.

One night, as Pris and I sat together, she let out a frustrated sigh and shook her head. "You won't believe what the neighbour said to me today."

I looked up from my laptop. "That bad?"

"She told me we're causing problems by paying our driver more than others do."

I frowned. "Why does she care what we pay him?"

"She thinks we're setting an expectation," Pris said. "I told her that our driver does more than just drive—he helps around the house, does repairs, and he built us a BBQ. And, by the way, John's a black belt in karate and speaks five languages, including English."

I chuckled. "Sounds like she should be paying her driver more and doesn't want to."

Pris didn't laugh. Instead, she pressed her lips together, then said, "Then she got to the real reason she was here."

I could tell by the look in her eyes that I wasn't going to like it.

"She told me MacKenzie shouldn't be spending time with the children of the servants." Her voice was steady, but I knew her well enough to hear the anger beneath it. "She meant Devi."

I sat up straighter. "She actually said that?"

Pris nodded, then exhaled. "It brought back memories. When I was a kid, my mother was obsessed with the idea of class. We weren't well off. She acted like we were above certain people. She told us who we could and couldn't play with, and I hated it."

She paused for a moment, eyes distant, searching her memory. "I don't even remember a particular name—just that it was always them, the kids who lived on the other side of the train tracks. That was all that mattered to her."

Pris let out a small, bitter laugh. "I still remember the way that felt. I was the oldest child, so she always told me I had to set the right example for my sisters. I never believed the way she did. I never chose my friends based on who they were or what they did. And that experience—it only made me more determined to stand by what I believed."

She glanced at me, her jaw set. "So, when this woman told me MacKenzie shouldn't be around Devi, all I could think was, I will not do that to my daughter."

I nodded slowly.

"Again, I politely, yet very firmly, told her that we trusted MacKenzie to choose her friends and that we don't see people through the same lens she does. Then I ended the conversation."

I leaned back, letting out a breath. "Good."

Pris nodded, then sat for a moment, staring ahead. "MacKenzie doesn't need us to tell her what's right. She already knows."

Devi continued spending time with MacKenzie and with us. Though there were always unspoken undercurrents of class and expectation around us, she moved forward with determination.

## When Pris Nearly Walked Away

This wasn't the only challenge Pris encountered. She had her own reckoning with biases too—and it nearly ended our time in India. It wasn't just one bad night. It was a rupture. One of the hardest, most defining moments in our marriage.

Not long after we had settled in, we were invited to the managing director's home for dinner. The meal was elaborate, the welcome gracious. After dinner, the men remained in the living room to talk business, while the wives moved into the kitchen to chat.

As an executive in the company, Pris stayed beside me.

At one point, the managing director came around with a coffee pot, topping up everyone's cup—until he reached Pris. He paused, then deliberately skipped her.

Without hesitation, she said, "I'll have some more, Ramu."

He blinked, visibly thrown, and replied awkwardly, "Why don't you go join the wives in the kitchen?"

She didn't say a word. Just turned and looked at me. And in that look, I knew it was time to leave. I made a polite excuse, and we walked out.

She didn't speak a single word the entire ride home—not with John, our driver in the front seat. But her silence was deafening. She was holding it in, every bit of it, until we got inside.

The moment the door shut behind us, it erupted.

"He skipped me. Deliberately. Like I didn't exist. And then told me where I belonged?" Her voice cracked with fury. "Do you have any idea how humiliating that was?"

I tried to soften it. "It was awful, I know. But maybe it was just a cultural—"

She whirled to face me. "Don't use culture as an excuse. Respect is universal."

I stepped back. "I'm not defending it. I just mean—maybe he didn't know how it would come across—"

"You don't get it!" she shouted. "You're a man. You've never had to make yourself smaller just to be heard. You've never had to measure your voice, your ambition, your presence—just to be allowed to stay in the conversation."

I was scrambling to fix it. "Pris, this is your moment. You can lead. You can change this."

She looked at me, eyes blazing. "I've already changed it, Ed. I've fought through the 1970s and 1980s. I've had my ideas dismissed, my tone policed, my presence questioned. I am done fighting to be allowed to lead. If this is what staying looks like—being erased, being told to go sit in the kitchen—then no. I'm not staying."

I didn't know what to say. I wanted to stay. I was certain in what we came to do. But I also wanted my wife to feel whole, seen, safe. And I didn't know if we could have both.

We barely spoke for weeks. The tension between us sat in the room like a third person.

And then, slowly, it shifted.

She didn't make a grand declaration. There was no dramatic breakthrough. Just a fierce resolve that took shape over time.

She chose to stay—but not out of compromise. She stayed on her terms. Not for them. Not for me. For herself.

And she did exactly what she said she would do.

She pushed the boundaries. Thoughtfully. Strategically. Persistently.

Over the months that followed—and through the years to come—Pris built something extraordinary. She led diversity and inclusion initiatives across India, China, and beyond. She created and delivered programmes that gave voice to women who had been kept waiting in the wings. She did it in ways that honoured culture while challenging its limitations—because she wanted the change to last.

She didn't ask for space. She shaped it around her. And in doing so, she left behind something far more enduring than a title or a policy—she left behind a legacy.

That night could have broken us. Instead, it became the beginning of a far more powerful impact.

## A Knock at the Door

One evening, three years later, everything changed.

When I opened the door, Devi was standing there—her face blotchy, breath uneven, eyes red-rimmed from crying. She wasn't one who showed emotions. She carried herself with strength, always. And yet, here she was, barely holding herself together.

Pris stepped forward at once, her voice filled with concern. "Devi, what happened?"

Devi shook her head, unable to speak. Her little hands were twisting together, her shoulders trembling slightly.

"Come inside," Pris said gently, placing a hand on her back and leading her to the couch. She sat beside her, waiting—patient and steady.

MacKenzie and I exchanged glances, both unsure of what had happened. Whatever it was, it had shaken her deeply.

We did not press her for answers. We let her sit in silence, breathing, gathering herself. The only sound in the room was the occasional sniffle as she tried and failed to hold back tears.

Minutes passed before she finally took a shaky breath and whispered, "I cannot go to school anymore."

Pris leaned in. "Why?"

Devi swallowed hard, gripping the fabric of her dress.

"My school fees," she murmured, her voice barely audible. "We are not able to pay."

She looked down, ashamed—as if speaking the words made the situation more real. Quickly, she wiped her face, determined not to cry again.

"School fee due for the past three months," she said softly. "The Principal told me and my brother not to come back until we clear the dues. My mother hasn't received her salary yet …"

Her voice cracked as tears welled up. "I didn't know what to do," she whispered, finally letting herself cry.

Something inside my chest tightened.

She wasn't asking for help. She wasn't pleading. She didn't expect anything from us. She came because she had no other place to go.

Pris reached for her hand. "Devi …" she started softly.

Devi shook her head quickly, cutting her off. "It is okay," she said, forcing a wobbly smile. "I just—I just wanted to tell you."

It wasn't okay.

That night, we sat together in silence for a long time.

For us, it was a small thing. A decision that would not change our lives in any significant way.

For Devi, it was everything.

Over time, we had come to understand her world—the tiny room she shared with her mother, sister, and cousin; the early mornings spent completing chores before the sun had even risen; the nights spent studying under a streetlight because their home was too dark.

And we had learned about her dream—not to escape, not to chase after wealth or status, but simply to continue. To not be stopped by things beyond her control.

That night, she thought her future was gloomy.

# Part 3

# Changing Each Other's Lives

"Everyone has a purpose in life and a unique
talent to give to others."

—Dr. Kallam Anji Reddy

# Chapter 10

# The Turning Point

When MacKenzie asked me to come over, I thought maybe I had said too much.

My stomach tightened the moment I stepped through the door. Pris Aunty and Ed Uncle were sitting in the living room. MacKenzie was sitting cross-legged on the couch, her eyes shining like she was keeping a big secret. She caught my eye and gave me a quick smile—reassuring, familiar. Somehow, it made me feel a little less afraid to sit.

I was nervous. I did not know why they had called me over, and a part of me was worried assuming maybe I had done something wrong by telling them. Maybe I had gone too far.

Pris Aunty smiled at me, soft and warm. "Devi, we wanted to talk to you about your school."

I swallowed, my heart pounding. "Yes?"

She took my hand gently. "We are going to take care of your school fees."

I did not understand at first.

I stared at her, blinking. "What?" I whispered.

Ed Uncle nodded. "We will pay your tuition fee. You don't have to worry about it anymore."

It felt like someone had knocked the air out of me. My hands clenched into fists in my lap. I looked down, afraid that if I said yes, I'd lose something I couldn't name. No one had ever offered me this kind of help before—and I didn't know how to receive it.

I whispered, "I don't know how to thank you."

Pris Aunty smiled. "You don't need to. Just keep going."

And then Uncle said something I'll never forget: "We believe in you, Devi."

I nodded, feeling like my throat was on fire. "I will. I promise."

MacKenzie grinned. "And you're not getting out of it that easily—I'm still making you help me with my maths homework."

I let out a small chuckle before I could stop it.

## A Foreign Car at My School

The next morning, Pris Aunty said they would take me to the school.

I had never been dropped off in a car before.

I didn't say much that morning, but something inside me felt different. Not lighter—just steadier, like I had been given a reason to keep going.

We drove through the streets of Hyderabad, past fruit vendors arranging their carts, past women in bright saris carrying baskets on their heads, past children in uniforms walking to school. I kept my hands folded on my lap, my heart racing. The car's air conditioning was cool. I still felt a nervous heat creeping up my neck.

As we were nearing the school, I saw other students through the gates—talking, laughing, jostling as they waited for the bell to ring. And then, when the car slowed down, they all stopped.

One by one, they turned.

Heads up, eyes wide.

Foreigners—with me.

## Breaking Barriers, Embracing Possibility

A hush fell over the courtyard.

Boys, dressed in crisp white shirts and navy shorts, paused mid-game, their laughter fading. A few still held their makeshift cricket bats, their eyes darting between us and their friends, unsure whether to continue playing or keep watching. Girls in neatly pressed skirts, their hair braided and tied with ribbons, whispered in groups, their glances flickering between me and Pris Aunty. Some peeked from behind doorways and pillars, wide-eyed, whispering urgently, trying to understand why we were here.

Teachers stood near the courtyard's edge, exchanging glances, their expressions unreadable.

For a moment, everything seemed to pause, the usual energy of the school replaced by curiosity, uncertainty, and something else—something I could not quite understand.

The moment we stepped forward, the whispering began again.

This wasn't just any school. The children here came from families who had sacrificed a lot to be  within these walls. Most of them were from modest homes, where every rupee counted, and sending a child to a private school—no matter how basic—was a sacrifice. Parents scraped together what they could, choosing this over the overcrowded government schools where classrooms overflowed beyond capacity, where teachers were stretched thin, and where learning was more of a struggle than a privilege.

Here, in this small yet proud institution, education was a lifeline.

Each morning, before lessons began, students gathered in neat rows, their white and navy uniforms forming an unbroken wave of blue and ivory. They stood with disciplined precision, their hands folded behind their backs as teachers made announcements, their voices echoing off the concrete walls. It was a routine, a ritual, a moment of unity before the day began.

Today, the attention wasn't on the morning assembly. It was on us.

A bell clanged in the distance—sharp, metallic—signalling the start of another school day. Teachers stepped out into the courtyard, some with their arms crossed, others looking on with curiosity.

I kept my eyes low, my fingers curling tightly around the edge of my uniform. I wanted to disappear, to shrink into the background. There was nowhere to hide.

The courtyard bustled with movement, students shifting in place, whispering behind cupped hands. Some stood near the balconies of the classrooms above, leaning against the railings for a better look. The school's open-air design made it impossible to blend in.

Inside, the classrooms were simple, looking out onto the courtyard with wooden doors left ajar to let in whatever breeze the morning had to offer. Rows of worn wooden benches filled the rooms, packed so tightly that students had little space to move. The walls, once vibrant, faded with time, bearing remnants of old lesson charts and timetables. A single ceiling fan spun lazily above, barely cutting through the warm air.

As we walked through the courtyard, teachers peeked from their classrooms, watching us with measured expressions. Their gazes flickered from Pris Aunty to Ed Uncle, to me. I wondered how many of them had ever seen something like this—foreigners stepping into their world, not as visitors, not as tourists, but for me.

We reached the Principal's office.

She was a short, pleasantly plump woman clad in a crisply starched sari, every pleat in place, her hair drawn back into a no-nonsense bun that spoke of discipline and purpose. A large bindi and vermilion adorned the centre of her forehead—a symbol of both tradition and authority. As she sorted through a stack of papers on her desk, her gold bangles clinked softly with each movement, creating a gentle rhythm that echoed through the room.

Her smile, when it came, was warm and welcoming, the kind that put you at ease. But her eyes—her eyes were sharp, inquisitive. There was something in her gaze that lingered, as though she was trying to read more than just my admission form.

And then, everything changed.

She looked up and noticed who was standing behind me. For a brief moment, everything froze. Her expression changed. A pause. Her eyes widened just a little, and she looked at me, then at them, and then back at me again—this time with visible astonishment.

They had come without fanfare, without fuss, and quietly paid the entire fee for my 9th standard—mine, and also my brother Raja's. The full year's tuition fee, including the examination fees. It was a gesture that went far beyond mere charity. It was a lifeline for my mother, who had been carrying the weight of our education alone for so long.

The Principal sat still for a few moments, absorbing the magnitude of what had just transpired. Her smile returned, softer now, touched by something she couldn't quite name. She gave a slight nod, one of those small gestures that speak volumes, as if acknowledging something deeper than words could convey.

In that exchange, I understood something profound.

This moment wasn't only about school fees.

It was about something much larger.

It was about shattering invisible barriers—those walls that keep girls like me confined in the background, our dreams stifled before they are even spoken.

It was about daring to imagine a different future.

"This is Devi's sponsor family," she announced to the staff members who had gathered nearby, her voice measured and formal, as though she were rehearsing a line she had never spoken before.

I noticed the way the words seemed to hang in the air—heavy, unfamiliar.

Sponsor family.

The phrase felt so big. So official. Almost out of place in my world, where the idea of someone stepping forward for *me* had always felt like a faraway dream.

I had always blended in, never wanting to draw too much attention. Never imagining that someone might choose me—not out of obligation, but out of love.

Pris Aunty placed a gentle hand on my back—steadying me, grounding me. She didn't need to say much. In that familiar, tender tone of hers, she simply said, "We just want to make sure she has everything she needs."

I looked up at her, unsure, my dark eyes searching hers for reassurance.

And something shifted inside me.

This wasn't just about school uniforms or textbooks.

This was about being seen.

This was about *belonging*.

It was about breaking the barrier between what I had known and what was now possible.

I wasn't just a girl they were helping.

I was someone they cared about.

Someone whose future mattered.

And, not just to me—

## A Promise to Honour

I had always thought that kindness came with conditions. Nothing was ever given freely—not food, not safety, not love. Even education had always felt fragile to me—something that could be taken away at any moment.

This was different.

And so, I worked even harder.

The day I received my report card is etched in my memory like it happened just yesterday. My class teacher, a kind and stern woman with a no-nonsense air, called me to the front of the room. Her eyes sparkled as she handed me the report card, her smile wide and genuine.

"Devi," she said, her voice warm with pride, "you've secured first rank in the entire class. You should be very proud of yourself."

For a moment, I just stood there, holding the paper in my trembling hands. I was two years younger than everyone else in my class, and yet, I had done it.

It was more than just marks on a sheet. It was proof that all the late nights, all the early mornings, all the silent prayers, and every drop of effort I had poured into my studies had not gone in vain. It wasn't just success—it was proof that I belonged, even in a world that didn't expect me to.

I clutched that report card close to my chest, and in that moment, I made myself a silent promise:

I will not waste what they have given me.

I would honour it—with everything I had.

# Chapter 11

# Bridging the Divide

The night before we were to take Devi to school, sleep refused to come.

I kept telling myself it was a small act—just paying the fees, ensuring she didn't drop out. Nothing dramatic. Nothing worth losing sleep over.

But deep in the stillness of that Hyderabad night, as the ceiling fan hummed above and the city quieted outside, I knew better.

This moment mattered. Far more than I had allowed myself to acknowledge.

I had seen that flicker in Devi's eyes before—a silent dread, the kind that lives behind the eyes of children who know how quickly something precious can be taken.

It was a look I recognised too well. I had once seen it in the mirror, as a boy who learned to read the air in the room like others read textbooks—always alert, always waiting for the next blow, the next outburst, the next loss.

I closed my eyes, and the memories came rushing back—uninvited, unstoppable.

The sharp scrape of a chair dragging across the linoleum floor—my sister shifting, bracing for impact.

A plate hurled. The heavy clatter as it shattered.

My mother's gasp. The thud of a body crumpling to the ground.

My voice, shaking like a diya in the wind—"Please, Dad. Don't. I want to live."

The funeral. The dream.

Leaning over his casket, searching for peace in that final moment—

But his eyes opened. His hands reached. He choked.

Even during death, the terror hadn't left.

The funeral parlour's cold air bit into my skin.

And through it all, the mask on my face did not crack.

I swallowed hard and blinked at the ceiling, trying to chase the memories away. But they had already made themselves at home—settling deep, like dust in the corners of an old house.

For years, survival was the only prayer I knew. Education became my ticket out—the one thread of hope I could hold on to. I had pushed, scraped, and climbed my way forward, each step an act of defiance.

But even after reaching safety, the past clung to me like a shadow at dusk—refusing to let go.

That night, as I lay in the darkness, something shifted. I finally saw it clearly—this wasn't only Devi's story.

It was mine, too.

Some might think that beatings, fear, and shame belong to faraway places or forgotten times.

But here in India—and across the world—there are still children who tremble inside their own homes.

Who learns early that silence can be safer than truth.

The language may change, the streets may look different, but the fear? The silence? And the strength it takes to speak? That is universal.

I had spent a lifetime running—running from pain, from fear, from the shadows that crept in when the world went quiet at night.

But now, something inside me was beginning to shift.

Sitting beside Devi, I was no longer that trembling boy waiting for it to stop.

I wasn't just surviving.

I was choosing.

In helping her walk toward her future, I had unknowingly turned back to face the past I thought I'd buried long ago.

With every act of support, with every word of encouragement, I wasn't just helping her—I was rewriting my own story.

A story where I no longer lived in the shadows of yesterday, but stepped—slowly, cautiously—into the light.

Toward a self I had never dared to imagine.

A man who could breathe without fear.

Who no longer flinched at kindness.

Who was beginning to believe, perhaps for the first time, that he was worthy of peace.

That night was the last time the dream came to me.

In its place, a stillness. A soft release.

I thought I had been freed.

But perhaps, I was only just beginning to understand what true freedom really means.

## School Days

Morning light slipped past the edge of the curtain, casting long golden streaks across the floor. I stretched, half-expecting the usual heaviness to sit on my chest—but it never came. Despite just a few hours of sleep, I felt different—lighter, as though something inside had unknotted itself in the night.

For the first time in a while, as long as I could remember, I didn't wake up carrying ghosts. The usual tightness in my chest, the tangled burden of worries that lingered like smoke in my mind—they had lifted.

I took a long, deep breath. And for once, it didn't feel like a fight. It felt … easy. Free.

The past hadn't vanished. The pain hadn't magically dissolved.

But something was different.

Maybe it was the first whisper of release.

Maybe, after all these years, I was finally beginning to understand what it means to loosen one's grip on sorrow—and let it go.

As we made our way through the early morning streets of Hyderabad—past chai stalls setting up, temple bells ringing in the distance, and autos weaving through traffic—I watched Devi from the corner of my eye.

She sat silently, her hands folded tightly in her lap, her face a mask of calm too perfect for a child her age. But her fingers betrayed her—tensed and flexed, her knuckles pale. A storm beneath still waters.

I knew that feeling.

I knew what it meant to step into a world that didn't feel built for you, to wonder if you belonged—or if everyone around you was silently asking the same thing.

I remembered it vividly. Sitting in a classroom I was never meant to be in. A professor placing a textbook in front of me, half-dismissive, half-curious.

"If you're going to sit here, you might as well try to follow."

Equations. Logic. A language that didn't shout or strike—it simply made sense.

I finished the semester's work in three weeks.

A scholarship followed. Then, a path out.

Yet the doubt—the ache of not truly belonging—never left.

But today, as I watched Devi sitting quietly beside me, I wasn't reliving it.

I was witnessing it unfold in real time. And for once, I wasn't alone in it.

When the school gates came into view, the atmosphere seemed to shift. A stillness settled over the courtyard. Heads turned. Eyes followed.

Whispers floated like incense smoke.

Devi kept her gaze low, her fingers curling tightly into the hem of her uniform. Every movement in her body spoke the same message: Don't look at me. Let me disappear.

I knew that feeling all too well.

But today felt different.

Today, she wasn't alone. And neither was I.

The principal's voice rang out across the compound. "This is Devi's sponsor family."

The words hung heavy in the air—formal, unfamiliar. Devi tensed.

Pris placed a hand gently on her back. "We just want to make sure she has everything she needs to succeed."

Devi paused. Then slowly, she looked up.

And in that simple act—chin lifted, eyes searching—I saw it.

This wasn't about school fees.

This was about breaking the kind of silence that passes down through generations.

It was about making sure she never again had to wonder if her future could be snatched away.

It was about giving her something I had never allowed myself to believe I was worthy of:  real chance.

For most of my life, I had felt like a stranger inside my own story. No matter the milestones, no matter how far I ran from my past, a voice always whispered: Do you truly belong?

That doubt shadowed every success, every moment of grace, making me question what I had earned, and whether I had earned anything at all.

But Devi?

I wanted her to know—in her bones, in her breath—that she was enough.

That she belonged to every room she entered.

That her worth wasn't up for debate.

This wasn't just about school. Or even opportunity.

It was about planting a seed so deep that she would never again question whether she mattered.

I had spent a lifetime trying to hush that question inside myself.

Maybe—just maybe—by walking beside her, I was finally answering it.

## Breaking Barriers Beyond the Classroom

A few weeks after Devi's first day at school, we returned—not just to check in on her, but to offer something more.

I had always believed that education was the great equaliser. It had lifted me from a place I thought I would never escape. It has given me direction, dignity, and the tools to rebuild a life. Now, it was time to pay that forward.

We arranged for a small donation—second-hand laptop computers, ones that still had life left in them.

When we rolled up to the school gates, word spread like wildfire. Excited murmurs turned into laughter and squeals as the children ran to the courtyard. We unloaded the laptops while wide-eyed students whispered in awe.

For many of them, a computer was something out of a film or textbook—glimpsed, never touched. Their world was ruled by chalk, slate, and handwritten margins filled with borrowed pens.

The school had no computer lab, so the principal suggested placing them in the library—a humble space lined with dog-eared books and dreams. It was the heart of the school, where a few hungry minds gathered to read beyond the syllabus. Now, it would beat louder.

Teachers and senior students pitched in to help—wiping desks, untangling cords, lining up the machines in a row. There weren't many, just enough to form a tiny island of possibility.

When the first screen flickered to life, the room fell silent. One small boy gasped. Another girl covered her mouth in awe. Older students exchanged nervous glances, unsure whether they were allowed to touch.

The teachers, too, leaned in with curiosity. Most had never used a computer before. They had grown up with chalkboards and dictation, but they knew the world beyond the school walls was changing fast. If they could learn, they could pass it on.

Devi and I knelt beside a few of the younger children. We showed them how to hold the mouse, how to click, how to type their names slowly—letter by letter—into a blank document.

Their fingers hovered at first, hesitant. But soon, the room filled with the soft tapping of keys. Giggles. The glow of recognition as their own names appeared on the screen—clear, crisp, real.

For these children, even attending school was a miracle—made possible by families who skipped meals or sold small possessions to keep them enrolled. Many had never seen a computer up close, let alone touched one.

And now, the door was open.

The principal stood, taking it all in. Her eyes brimmed with pride and something else—hope.

"This will change everything," she whispered.

And as I looked around that little library—once just a haven for readers, now a portal into the future—I saw it, too.

This wasn't just about technology.

It was about access. Dignity.

A step toward empowerment—for those who had always been told they couldn't.

# Chapter 12

# The Other Side of the Gates

My mother stopped working for Raji Madam in 2009. Suddenly, I found myself on the outside.

The transition was abrupt, as if a door had slammed shut in my face, without a word of warning. Before, I had moved freely through that world, slipping past the guards with a nod, my presence unquestioned. I belonged there—or at least, I thought I did.

Standing at the towering gates of their community, I was just another outsider, pleading for access that would never be granted.

I stood there for hours, watching every car that approached, my heart racing each time a vehicle slowed near the entrance. Maybe it was them. Maybe they would see me. Maybe they would stop.

I imagined their surprise, their smiles—the warmth of Ed Uncle's voice calling out, "Devi!" and Pris Aunty hurrying up, arms open wide.

I clung to those visions as the hours dragged on, as the sun beat down harshly on my back, as fatigue crept into my bones.

The guards didn't care. They didn't even bother to look up anymore.

At first, I spoke gently. I folded my hands. Tried in English. Then Telugu.

"Please, *nenu vaalla sneehithini* (I'm their friend). They'll want to see me."

They exchanged glances, amused. One of them leaned back in his chair and muttered, "*Aithe vallu pilustaru* (then they will call)."

If they wanted to see you, they'd call you. Madam must be busy.

I came back again. And again. Even when the rains started, soaking through my kurta, puddles forming under my feet.

They stopped responding altogether.

One day I heard them laugh when I walked away.

"Rojulu *kaayam ayyayi. Ippatiki ardam kaledu?* (it's been days, and she *still* doesn't get it?)"

Days have passed. Still haven't figured it out?

I wanted to scream, but I didn't. I tucked myself in and waited—across the road, by the wall, where I could watch the gate and pretend hope was enough.

The longer I waited, the more my hope unraveled like a frayed thread.

Did they know I was here?

Had they forgotten me?

Had I imagined it all—the affection, the warmth, the belonging?

They had always made me feel like I mattered.

They always called me Devi—not beta, not child, not something vague. Just me. My name.

And yet, here I was.

Alone. Drenched. Invisible.

Then, just as I was ready to give up—really give up—I saw a familiar figure step out of the gate.

John bhaiya. Their driver. My heart surged.

I jumped up, nearly slipping on the slick stone.

"John bhaiya!" I called, my voice breaking.

"Dayachesi ... please tell them I've come. I've been waiting ... every day."

He stopped. Took me in—my sunburnt skin, cracked lips, eyes heavy with too many sleepless nights.

His face changed. Just slightly.

"I'll tell them," he said. Not unkind.

I nodded, breath caught in my chest. I wanted so badly to believe him.

But a part of me, quiet and cruel, whispered: What if I had been wrong all along?

I had been carrying so many silent goodbyes—I never said out loud. Not even to myself.

Like how Nana had stopped calling. Stopped writing.

How his absence slipped into our lives like a shadow—until one day, it just stayed.

When I was in tenth standard, we got the call. He had died.

Amma didn't cry—not in front of us.

Jyothi was quiet for days.

And me?

I didn't know how to mourn someone who had already disappeared long before his body did.

But standing outside those gates, hoping someone would remember me, I realised how deeply those old absences still echoed inside me.

I had lost people before. I just hadn't expected to lose them again.

As John's car disappeared through the gates, I stayed rooted in place. Watching. Waiting.

## When Hope Comes Home

It started with the sound of an engine—smoother, deeper than the usual hum of the street.

In our neighbourhood, the world moved on foot, on rickety bicycles, in sputtering auto-rickshaws that weaved through the chaos like fish in a crowded stream. Motorcycles zipped past, honking impatiently, navigating the maze of people and stray dogs. The air was alive with voices—vendors shouting their prices, mothers calling their children, the clang of metal pots against stone.

So, when a shiny, tan-coloured Honda CR-V rolled onto our narrow road, it was as if the entire street held its breath.

Heads turned. Conversations faltered. The car gleamed unnaturally under the harsh sun, out of place among the dust and simple homes. Neighbours whispered behind doorways and half-drawn curtains.

I ran to the doorway, breath caught between hope and disbelief.

Could it be?

John bhaiya stepped out—not in a uniform, not with a cap, just as he always had. He never needed one. He was part of their world, yet never distant, never made to feel lesser. He moved with familiarity, his steps unhurried as he walked to the back of the car.

My heart pounded as the door opened, and then—Ed Uncle and Pris Aunty came.

For months, I had imagined this moment. I had told myself they would come. That they hadn't forgotten.

As the weeks had stretched into months, doubt had crept in like an unwelcome guest, whispering that maybe I had been wrong. That maybe I was just a fading memory, a name they had once spoken with kindness but no longer carried in their hearts.

Yet here they were.

Standing in the dust of our narrow lane, under the watchful eyes of a neighbourhood that had never seen visitors like them before, they didn't hesitate. They didn't look uncomfortable or uncertain.

They simply smiled.

Pris Aunty adjusted her sunglasses, taking in the surroundings with curiosity. Ed Uncle's gaze landed on me— his expression warm, familiar, like I belonged.

And then, there was Jasper.

The moment the car door opened, he sprang out, his tail wagging furiously, his excitement spilling over like an overflowing pot of chai. His small white paws skittered against the uneven pavement as he darted towards me, letting out an eager bark.

I barely had time to react before he reached me, his little body wriggling with pure joy.

"Jasper!" I laughed, crouching down as he leapt into my lap, licking my face with wild enthusiasm. He had always been thrilled to see me, as if every visit was the greatest moment of his life.

But when I glanced up, I saw Amma and Jyothi standing stiffly in the doorway, their hands pressed to their sides, their unease evident.

Amma had never been comfortable around dogs. Jyothi was even more wary, shifting behind her, eyes darting between Jasper and me.

Jasper—oblivious to their apprehension—turned his bright eyes towards them, his tail still wagging. He took a small, hopeful step forward.

"Vaddu, Jasper!" Jyothi whispered sharply, stepping back with wide eyes.

Amma reached for the edge of her sari, twisting the fabric between her fingers, her discomfort visible.

Pris Aunty must have noticed. She stepped forward, scooping Jasper into her arms before he could bound toward them. "Come here, little one," she murmured, scratching behind his ears. He settled instantly, but his eyes remained fixed on me, as if waiting for permission to greet the others.

A silence echoed between us.

Would Amma and Jyothi see Jasper the way I did? Would they ever trust his harmless, loving nature?

Before the weight of that thought could settle, Ed Uncle spoke, his voice easy, light. "Jasper has been waiting to see Devi. I think she's his favourite."

A slow warmth spread through me.

Like it didn't matter.

Like we mattered.

I swallowed, my throat tight with something I couldn't name, and stepped aside, allowing them in.

## Quiet Promises

Inside, our home was as simple as it had always been—small, the air thick with afternoon heat, the ceiling fan creaking as it struggled to provide relief. Amma had set out our best plastic chairs, their colours dulled by time, and I felt a flicker of shame.

Ed Uncle and Pris Aunty sat down without a second thought, as if this space was no different from their own.

Amma emerged with two cups of chai, her hands steady despite the nervousness in her eyes. She wasn't used to serving guests like these—guests who had once lived in a world so different from ours.

They accepted the tea with easy smiles, sipping without hesitation. Their presence filled the small space with something I hadn't realised I had been missing—belonging.

They had come. For me. For us.

That day stayed with me long after they moved back to America. Though they returned to India often and I saw them from time to time, life had a way of pulling us in different directions.

In that moment, they had made something clear: I had never been forgotten. I had never been left behind.

Some bonds are stronger than distance. Some relationships exist beyond walls.


## Higher Education and Continued Support

Before they left Hyderabad in 2009, Ed Uncle even offered to take my brother Raj to the USA for a better education, but my Amma were hesitant to let him go. Looking back, we sometimes wished we had trusted him more.

As I moved into higher education, my school suggested that I continue at Sri Chaitanya College, one of the most prestigious institutions in Hyderabad. Around that time, communicating with them became difficult—I had no mobile phone, I was no longer their neighbour, and as per the colony's rules, I could not enter anymore.

Yet, they made sure I had what I needed.

Before they left, they visited my college and paid ₹ 20,000 to cover my entrance fees so I could start there.

It was heart-breaking to see them go. They had been more loving and supportive than many people we knew, treating us like family without expecting anything in return.

Nobody else encouraged me to pursue my education. Everyone—including my family—thought I should get married.

Ed Uncle and Pris Aunty made me promise I would finish school.

# Chapter 13

# The Ripple Effect of Kindness

The first time we went to Siria Orphanage, it was a scorching afternoon. The compound was weathered and worn, yet full of life—135 children, each one carrying their own story. Laughter echoed across the yard, mixed with whispers and the occasional quiet tear.

We always brought Jasper, our little Schnoodle. He would dart across the courtyard, chasing invisible butterflies and drawing bursts of joy from the children. MacKenzie would kneel beside even the shyest ones, gently coaxing them to come forward and touch his curly fur. One tiny girl, no older than six, whispered, "Bhaiyya (brother), I've never touched a dog before," and then pressed her cheek against Jasper, eyes shining with wonder.

At night, the dormitories were crowded. Thin mats pulled out from cardboard boxes, each carefully marked with a child's name. By day, the same rooms transformed into classrooms, the scratch of chalk echoing off tired blackboards. Twice a week, the children would line up for a bath under the cold-water hose—some giggling, others shivering in silence.

It was on one of those early visits that we noticed a boy standing quietly by the back wall. Ten years old, thin, alert, always watching but never approaching. His fingers on one hand were fused—burn scars from long ago, never properly treated.

Each time we came, I would smile and greet him. He gave a small nod in return but stayed at a distance.

Then one afternoon, while MacKenzie was holding an English class in the verandah, I saw him watching Jasper with a focused gaze. I slowly walked over, Jasper trotting beside me.

"You like him?" I asked softly. Our driver, John, translated for him into Telugu—"Nuvvu āyanni istapadutunnāva?" After a pause, the boy replied, "Jasper santōsanga kanipistunnādu (Jasper looks happy.)"

He reached out hesitantly with his scarred hand. Jasper sniffed it, then gently licked his fingers. A flicker of something passed across the boy's face—not quite a smile, but something softer. In that quiet moment, it wasn't just a boy meeting a dog. It felt like two souls recognising each other's silent pain.

We didn't know his full story yet.


## Circles of Joy

One of the children's favourite games was the "Fruit Salad Song." The moment we arrived, their faces would light up. We all gathered in a big circle as someone shouted "Watermelon!" and everyone stretched their arms wide. Then "Papaya!" with oval shapes, and "Banana-nana-nana," with dramatic peeling motions. Finally, we would chant together, "Fruit salad! Fruit salad!" while pretending to stir invisible bowls. The air would fill with laughter.

These were more than just games. Such activities became rituals of belonging. In those moments, the old concrete walls of the orphanage seemed to soften. There was no hierarchy, no separation—just people, children and adults, moving together in a shared spirit.

Every weekend, we loaded the car with fresh mangoes, bananas, and oranges. The children would rush toward us, eyes gleaming—not only for the fruits, but for the break from routine, the joy of connection, and the comfort of being seen.

Over time, these weekends became something deeper. Our friendship grew stronger. We were all learning—children and adults alike—what it truly meant to show up with open hands and open hearts.

Whenever possible, we would take five boys or five girls home with us for the night—never mixing the groups. They entered the house slowly, eyes wide, taking in every detail. A warm, home-cooked meal felt like a grand feast. At first, they would eat hesitantly, unsure of what was allowed. But soon, not a scrap of food remained on any plate.

After dinner, they took hot water baths—unimaginable luxuries for children who were used to cold hosepipes. We'd show them how to turn the knobs, and they'd laugh in disbelief. Later, wrapped in soft towels, they'd sit on the carpet watching cartoons, eyes wide, mouths open in wonder.

The next morning, we'd take them to a local clinic for medical and dental check-ups. Even the sharp smell of antiseptic couldn't wipe the excitement off their faces. They'd flip through colourful magazines, whispering to each other, pointing at the pictures.

Then lunch was planned at a restaurant—it was their first such experience. The way they looked at the idlis, dosas, and ice creams was full of awe. Every expression reminded us of all the things we had taken for granted.

We would drop them back in the evening, always staying a little longer—singing songs, sharing stories, playing games before saying goodbye.

Then, one weekend, Prashanth's name appeared on the list.

## Scars That Speak

He was ten—quiet, watchful. I had already noticed the fused fingers on his right hand. After dinner that evening, I gently asked him about it. He replied in Telugu, with John translating for us.

When he was just two or three, a spark from faulty wiring threw him across the room. His fingers were badly burned, and over time, they fused together. No one had taken him to a doctor.

He shared this like it wasn't thing—no sadness, no anger, just plain facts.

Something inside me stirred.

Suddenly, I was six years old again.

It was a bitterly cold day in Chicago. The older kids were skating on the frozen creek—I wasn't allowed to join. So I wandered off towards a neighbour's garbage fire. I threw in a stick just to see it burn. An ember landed on my nylon jacket. In seconds, it caught fire. I screamed and tried to remove it, but the material had already melted into my skin.

A neighbour saw me. He pushed me into the snow and poured ice over me until the flames calmed down. My skin blistered. At the hospital, they said I would need skin grafts.

My mother never left my side. She was there—soothing, encouraging, present.

My father came once or twice. He stayed distant. Cold. He believed it was my fault.

Then my class one teacher arrived. I still don't know how she found out, but she came with books and offered kindness. She read to me when I couldn't. She made sure I didn't fall behind.

Her presence said, *You matter. You have a future.*

But once I returned home, everything was the same. My father's temper came back like nothing had changed. I remember one night—I must have said something casual. He slapped me so hard my ears rang.

That's when I realised—My near-death experience hadn't changed his low opinion of me.

So I started hiding everything. I buried the pain. I smiled. I pretended. I stayed silent.

And now, sitting with Prashanth, I felt that silence begin to crack.

He wore no mask. There was pain in his story, yes—but also the joy of a child still open to the world.

Without thinking, I lifted my shirt slightly and showed him the scars on my back.

"I have scars too," I said gently. "From a fire."

He looked up at me, wide-eyed. Then slowly reached out, his fingertips grazing my skin.

We didn't speak. We didn't need to.

Something passed between us. It wasn't about comparing wounds. It was about being seen.

And being seen—that is where healing begins.

## A Hand Reclaimed

We took him to a free medical camp where Doctors Without Borders were offering surgeries for children with injuries and birth defects. Families stood in long queues under the harsh sun. Mothers rocked babies with cleft lips. Fathers held the hands of little ones with burn scars and twisted limbs.

Prashanth clung to my side, his eyes scanning the queue of bandaged children. His small fingers gripped my sleeve.

"Will it hurt a lot?" he asked, voice barely a whisper.

I knelt beside him, placing a hand on his shoulder. "Maybe a little. But these doctors are very good. We'll be right here with you."

John, our driver, added, "They'll treat your hand, beta. You'll be able to play without pain."

When our turn came, a kind doctor examined his fused fingers with care.

"He's a good candidate," he said. "We can help."

The surgery was scheduled at Apollo Hospital. The surgeon showed us the X-rays and explained the procedure. "We'll restore movement," he said. "But aftercare is crucial— daily cleaning, regular exercises, and close monitoring to prevent infection."

Pris and I didn't hesitate.

On the morning of the surgery, Prashanth was quiet. It was his first time in a hospital like this. No one had ever cared about his injury—let alone offered to fix it.

As the nurses prepared him, he looked up and asked in Telugu, *"Nuvvu vachesava?"* (You won't leave me, right?)

"I'll be right here," I said. "Aunty and I are not going anywhere."

Hours later, the surgeon met us in the corridor, the smell of antiseptic still hanging in the air. Prashanth was groggy, his hand neatly wrapped in fresh white bandages.

"How soon does he need a check-up?" I asked.

Pris added, "We're planning to take him back tomorrow—but we'll come regularly for follow-ups."

The doctor shook his head. "Not possible. If he goes back now, there's a high risk of infection. He needs clean surroundings and consistent wound care."

Devi translated the doctor's words into Telugu. Prashanth nodded slightly, eyes half-closed.

Pris and I exchanged a glance. That was enough.

"He'll stay with us," I said.

And just like that, our home became his place of healing.

## The Road to Recovery

The next six weeks tested all of us. Each morning, we cleaned his wound, changed the dressing, and checked for signs of infection. Physiotherapy was the hardest. His little fingers—stiff from years of immobility—resisted every movement.

But he never complained.

Even when the pain brought tears, he swallowed them back. He was determined to heal.

Devi came often. She would sit quietly beside him, a steady, calming presence. She understood him in a way none of us fully could—maybe because she too had grown through hardship.

She translated his thoughts, switching effortlessly between Telugu and English, making sure we understood his fears, his hopes, and every small step of progress. But more than that—she listened.

She made him feel safe enough to speak.

"*Nuvvu chesi chudadhu. Nenu venaka nunchi unnanu.*" (Don't worry, just try. I'm right here.)

At first, he hesitated—used to silence, used to enduring everything on his own. But Devi wouldn't let him retreat. She coaxed him out gently, showing him that strength isn't only about being tough—it's also about letting someone stand beside you.

A shift started taking place.

A boy who had learnt to disappear slowly began to show himself. He was learning that vulnerability wasn't weakness— it was where real healing started. Through her care, Devi gave him the language of trust.

Our home slowly transformed. It wasn't just MacKenzie's music or Jasper's barking that filled the air anymore. There was a quieter energy—one of patience, of resilience.

MacKenzie treated him like a little brother—bringing him chai, teaching him how to use the TV remote. Jasper would sniff his bandages gently and then curl up at his feet, like a small furry guard.

We ensured he ate well, massaged his hand after therapy, and clapped for every small improvement in movement.

At first, his smiles were shy and fleeting. Then they became real.

One afternoon, when Jasper tried to steal food off his plate, Prashanth giggled and scolded him gently.

That's when I knew—he was healing on the inside too.

When the time came to send him back to the orphanage, a quiet heaviness came over me. It wasn't just the dusty road or narrow bylanes—it was knowing we weren't taking him back to a home, but to a system that barely noticed him.

In the back seat, he sat beside MacKenzie, stealing glances at me—searching for something on my face, a silent question, a quiet hope.

The orphanage hadn't changed. The same faded yellow walls, peeling paint, and that tired old iron gate.

The sharp scent of Dettol still clung to his shirt—too clean, too fresh for a place like this. The air inside smelled of damp clothes, steel vessels, and dreams that had no room to grow. Some children came running, overjoyed to see Prashanth. Others sat quietly in corners. The lone caretaker looked worn out, her sari slipping off her shoulder, eyes dull with exhaustion.

Prashanth held my hand tightly as we walked to the director's office—a cramped room with plastic chairs, piles of unlabelled files, and a fan that creaked overhead. The man behind the desk didn't bother to stand.

## The Price of a Child

"So, you've brought him back," he said flatly, without a trace of warmth.

Outside, Prashanth now held both my hands. "Do I have to stay?" he whispered.

Pris stood silently, lips pressed tight. MacKenzie stepped closer, shielding him instinctively.

I crouched beside him. "Let's just talk to the director, okay?"

Then John approached. "Sir, he's asking for money … to take Prashanth back."

I blinked. "What?"

"He said you've spoiled him. Now, if you want him to stay here, you'll have to pay."

I stood slowly, disbelief weighing heavy.

The director returned, more blunt this time. "You've made him soft by keeping him with you. If you want him here, pay. Otherwise … take him."

His eyes never met Prashanth's—only ours, calculating, like we were a walking ATM.

We had raised over ₹5 lakhs for this orphanage—sent supplies, shared their story abroad, even hosted a live webathon with songs, dances, and blessings. And now, this—turning a child into a transaction.

Pris and I exchanged a look. No words were needed.

I turned to Prashanth, placed a hand on his shoulder. "Come. We're going."

The director didn't protest. He scowled and waved us off—clearly disappointed that the money train had ended.

Back at the car, MacKenzie leaned in and whispered to Prashanth, "You're my brother now."

He exhaled shakily, like he'd been holding his breath since we arrived.

## The Spoon He Kept

A simple errand brought back a piece of his past we never expected.

John, our driver, was going to pick up his son for a birthday party when Prashanth suddenly sat upright, forehead pressed to the car window, eyes fixed.

"John Uncle … my Aunty lives here," he said softly. "I know this street."

John immediately called me. "Sir, what should I do?"

"Stop the car. Knock on the door," I said.

He pulled over beside a modest house with chipped green paint and a tall mango tree in the courtyard.

A woman opened the door, confused at first—until she saw Prashanth.

"Prashanth?" she said, astonished.

As they spoke, John learned something none of us had known—his mother and sister were alive. About a year ago, in desperation, they had placed him in the orphanage, hoping he'd have a better life and access to education.

That evening, Prashanth sat at home, deep in thought. He took the number his aunt gave him and dialled. It rang twice.

"Hello?" came a woman's voice.

He held the phone tightly. "Amma," he said, barely audible.

There was a pause. Then a sound—sharp, breathless, but no words.

Prashanth didn't cry. He never did. But his grip on the phone didn't loosen. His silence spoke volumes.

We arranged to meet her at a small restaurant the following weekend.


## He Called Her Amma

When we arrived, Prashanth stood still in the doorway. A woman sat by the window, fiddling with the edge of her dupatta. When her eyes met his, she stood abruptly.

"Prashanth!" she called out.

He walked straight to her, paused for just a moment, then rested his head lightly against her shoulder.

Her hands trembled as she held him close.

There were no dramatic tears. Just presence. Recognition. A bond that had endured.

Over lunch, we gently explained our wish to raise him and offer the care and education she had once hoped he'd receive at the orphanage.

She listened carefully. Then turned to him.

"Is this what you want?" she asked in Telugu.

Prashanth gave a small nod. "Yes, Amma. I want to stay with them."

Her eyes welled up, but she didn't cry either. She reached out and touched his cheek.

"*Naa bidda* ..." she whispered—my child. Then, turning to us, she added softly, "Take care of him."

# Chapter 14

# Navigating the Satyam Crisis

Earlier in this book, I mentioned that the story of Satyam wasn't the focus. Our time in India was about far more than a single company or a singular crisis.

I also know that curiosity is inevitable.

Satyam's name is still etched in business history, remembered as one of India's most infamous corporate scandals. Those who were part of it—employees, customers, and leaders alike—were forever changed. And we were two of them—Pris and I.

For that reason, I have chosen to share this segment. Not just to recount what happened, but to reflect on what it taught us about leadership, resilience, and human connection in times of crisis.

In January 2009, Satyam Computer Services was thrust into the spotlight when its chairman, B. Ramalinga Raju, confessed to a massive accounting fraud, admitting to falsifying revenues and assets totaling over $1 billion. The revelation led to Satyam being dubbed India's Enron, symbolising one of the country's most significant corporate scandals. *Business Week* ran a headline that summed it up best: From Icon to I Con. The financial and reputational collapse was swift and brutal.

When we moved our family from the USA to India, we trusted Ramalinga Raju. We trusted his vision. We uprooted our lives, embraced an entirely new culture, and committed ourselves fully to what we thought was a company built on integrity and innovation.

Between 2005 and 2009, Satyam's commitment to leadership excellence earned international recognition. The company established itself as a global pioneer in talent development. The initiatives we built became a model for other companies striving to create high-impact leadership programmes.

Satyam, the company so many had dedicated themselves to, was suddenly exposed as one of the largest corporate frauds in India's history. The sense of failure was overwhelming.

I had always prided myself on my ability to assess character, to choose my commitments wisely—yet here I was, standing in the wreckage of a company I had trusted in, watching the fallout unfold in real-time. Employees were in shock. Investors were outraged. Friends and colleagues questioned their own judgment, asking themselves how they had missed the warning signs.

For the first time in my career, doubt crept in with an intensity I had never known.

Had I made a terrible mistake? Had I misjudged everything?

## The Emotional Fallout: A Crisis Beyond Business

This wasn't just a financial scandal. It was a human catastrophe.

People were not just losing money—they were losing everything.

A senior executive who had given more than a decade of his life to Satyam sat across from me in a leadership coaching session, his hands trembling, tears rolling down his face. With just a year left before retirement, he had invested his life savings in Satyam stock—now worthless.

A thirty-year-old manager received a call from her father. "Resign immediately, beta, before your name is dragged into this. Before your reputation is also ruined." In India, a job is not just about income. It is reputation. It is about honour. When that foundation is shaken, it sends ripples through entire families.

A young professional, just weeks from his shaadi, found his engagement hanging by a thread. His fiancée's family, afraid of uncertainty, reconsidered the *rishta* (relationship/union).

For many employees, their lives were tied to Satyam's survival. Parents had taken loans to educate their children based on their salaries. Some had just bought homes, believing in the company's future.

Planned marriages were cancelled. Homes were sold. Futures were shattered.

And yet, something unexpected happened.

## A Culture That Endured Beyond the Crisis

Satyam was collapsing at the top, yet within the organisation, something remarkable was happening—the people stood together.

The bonds built over the years—the trust, the friendships, the shared purpose—remained unshaken. Employees stayed connected, continuing to support one another even as the crisis unfolded.

We have remained closely connected to our former colleagues, who have now become friends and our chosen family, attending dozens of reunions. As we left India, we created a time capsule, where team members shared their memories, dreams, and reflections on their journey. Five years later, when the time capsule was opened, those who had once been colleagues—now spread across industries and continents—came together once again to reflect on what our time together had meant to them.

Reunions continued through the years, the most recent when many travelled to America to attend Pris and my 35th wedding anniversary celebration. Another is planned for early 2026.

Through these reunions, we have witnessed the incredible resilience of those who once walked the halls of the company. We have seen careers flourish, families expand, and friendships stand the test of time. What began as professional relationships in India's most tumultuous corporate crisis has transformed into a lifelong network of support, shared memories, and unwavering encouragement.

Though Satyam as an institution collapsed, the spirit of its people never did. That legacy—the connections forged through both triumph and adversity—continues to thrive. The company may have fallen, but its people never did.

## A Shift in Leadership: From Strategy to Survival

The remaining leaders could not shy away from the hard truths.

Satyam was imploding. Employee morale was shattered. The uncertainty was suffocating. If there was to be a chance of survival, immediate action was needed.

At most companies facing such a crisis, leadership would focus on damage control—rebuilding brand image, reassuring investors, and containing legal exposure. None of that would matter if we did not take care of our people first.

Healing employees was the only way forward.

A structured plan was needed—not just for rebuilding the business, but also for helping people process their grief, their anger, their fear.

Satyam already had a pool of professionally trained internal coaches. They were given a new mission: to ensure that no employee felt abandoned. No one should feel like just another casualty of corporate fraud.

Among those leading this powerful movement was Pris. She went beyond frameworks and assessments—she listened. She built deep trust with employees at every level, particularly with the women, who often confided in her things they could not tell anyone else. She conducted one-on-one sessions across campuses, helping people face not just career uncertainty but personal heartbreak.

She helped organise career fairs, connected people with companies still hiring, and mentored those who had never written a résumé before. Under her guidance, along with the team, more than 20,000 employees either found new roles or discovered the confidence to pursue them. Pris didn't just coach people—she saw something in them, and in turn, they believed in themselves. In the midst of chaos, her presence was steady, calm, and respected—she was regarded not only as a leader, but as someone whom people looked at with reverence, a true guru.

## Lessons in Crisis Leadership

The biggest leadership lesson I learned from this experience was this: healing must come before performance.

If we did not address the pain our employees were feeling—the fear, the grief, the shattered trust—then no strategy, no restructuring, no new leadership could ever work. Rebuilding trust and restoring hope had to come first.

Communicate—even when there is nothing to say. Silence is the enemy of trust. Employees facing uncertainty will fill in the gaps with fear and misinformation. Too often, leaders assume that a single email or press release is enough. It is not. Face-to-face conversations matter. People need to hear from their leaders directly.

Acknowledge emotions—starting with your own. In a crisis, leaders are not immune to pain. I felt it myself. At first, I hesitated to show it—fearing it would make me seem weak. Employees do not need a leader who is invulnerable. They need a leader who is human. The more openly leaders address their own emotions, the more trust they build with their teams.

Fight misinformation with facts. The Indian press reported that Satyam had no cash to pay salaries. It was false. The leadership team knew that if customers accelerated payments, Satyam could cover payroll. Employees did not know that. When leaders do not actively combat rumours, fear takes over. Misinformation spreads quickly in moments of uncertainty. The only way to counter it is with clear, frequent, and factual updates.

Honesty is better than pretending to have all the answers. In a crisis, leaders often try to project certainty, even when they do not have it. That is a mistake. Employees do not expect leaders to know everything—honesty is expected. When circumstances are fluid, saying: "I do not know, though here is what I do know" is more reassuring than false confidence. People respect leaders who are transparent about what they know, what they are working toward, and what remains uncertain.

Despite all our efforts, Satyam could not recover alone.

In April 2009, just four months after the scandal, Tech Mahindra acquired Satyam for $1.2 billion through a government-overseen auction process led by the Indian authorities. The acquisition provided a financial lifeline and helped preserve thousands of jobs. Yet it came at a cost. The company's identity changed overnight. Thousands of employees were laid off. Many others chose to leave— unwilling to remain with a brand they no longer trusted.

The legacy of Satyam remains complicated. Its name will forever be associated with one of India's worst corporate betrayals.

Yet, in those dark months, something rare happened—we prioritised people over profit.

In times of extreme uncertainty, organisations that stand by their employees still find a way forward.

## Coming Full Circle: My Personal Transformation

At the time, it felt like one of the worst experiences of my life and career.

I had trusted the wrong person. I had moved my family across the world for a role that ended in scandal. I had watched a company I cared about implode under the weight of deception.

As time passed, clarity emerged.

India changed me.

It was in India that I learned the power of vulnerability in leadership. It was in India that I saw how resilience is not just about survival—it is about transformation.

Pris, too, found her own strength in the storm. Her courage and deep empathy helped hold others together when everything else was falling apart.

Even with everything that happened, we do not regret moving to India.

The lessons we learned—about crisis, resilience, and leadership—became the foundation of everything we teach today.

Satyam tested us in ways we never expected.

In the end, it wasn't the scandal that defined us—

It was how we chose to lead through it.

Our journey in India did not end with Satyam.

Nor with Devi's education.

Nor with bringing Prashanth home.

It continued—in every life we touched, and in the life that touched us back.

"Collage from the *bhoomi pooja* in late 2005, for the School of Leadership in Hyderabad, featuring Ed Cohen, his wife Pris, daughter MacKenzie, Satyam colleagues, and the Hindu priest conducting the rituals."

"Pris, Ed, and MacKenzie at a leadership retreat in Dubai, December 2006."

"Ed snapped this photo of a father picking up his children from school, while visiting Devi at her school in 2009."

"Ed with Devi and her cousin Raj at their school in 2007, during the visit when their fees were paid."

"Devi at her home, 2009."

"Ed with two children and his dog Jasper at the orphan school in Hyderabad."

"Pris with Prashanth (right) and three other boys from the orphanage during an excursion to Hyderabad airport to receive visitors."

"Ed with Prashanth during his time at boarding school near Hyderabad, 2010"

"Pris (centre) with the Satyam School of Leadership Team celebrating the Association for Talent Development #1 Best Award ranking, 2007."

"Devi at Microsoft, 2025 — a long way from her childhood studies under a streetlamp."

# Chapter 15

# We Said Goodbye,
# Then Returned

MacKenzie's graduation was both joyful and emotional—a true happy-sad moment. Her class had only eight students, but their stories spanned continents—India, Europe, Australia, and America. The school organised a simple dinner, filled with warmth and sincerity. Each student spoke from the heart.

When MacKenzie stood to speak, she held the room with confidence. Her voice was steady, her words full of gratitude.

"India has been more than a place for me—it's been a journey. I've traveled across this beautiful country, learned to cook real Indian curries (sometimes too spicy), and made friends I'll carry with me for life. Thank you for giving me a second home."

That evening wasn't just about graduation—it was the closing of a cherished chapter.

Later that night, around 10 p.m., we left for the airport. Our flight was at 2 a.m. Over thirty friends came in a caravan of cars, driving through the Hyderabad night one last time together. There was laughter, music, and the occasional silence. They weren't just there to drop us off—they were there to hold space for a goodbye that was heavy for all.

As we made our way toward immigration and turned back, they were still there—lined up behind the glass, still standing, still waving, their eyes following us. Not one of them had moved. They stayed until we turned the corner and were no longer visible.

It was one of those rare, sacred moments when you realise just how deep those relationships had become.

## Leaving Prashanth

Leaving Prashanth behind was one of the hardest decisions we ever had to make. He had become family. He had grown under our care, and his presence was irreplaceable. But taking him with us abroad was never possible. Even with affidavits or guardianship letters, without a birth certificate or Aadhaar-like document, we couldn't apply for a passport. Every door we tried was shut.

It wasn't a matter of choice—it was bureaucracy. Prashanth had no official birth record, which meant no passport, no visa, no legal way forward. His mother, who wanted only the best for him, gave her full support for us to raise him. Still, we had no path ahead.

We enrolled him in a boarding school, hoping it would offer structure and stability. But over time, it became clear the environment wasn't the right fit. Academics alone weren't enough. He needed a home. A support system. People who truly cared about his growth.

Our commitment to him never changed. We continued to return to India multiple times a year—checking in, guiding him through his ups and downs, and reminding him he was never alone. Eventually, we arranged for him to stay with our friends Nishi and David, fellow Americans. When they moved to the UK, he shifted to live with Nayana and her family.

Letting go was painful, even though we trusted his strength. He had already endured so much, yet remained determined.

School was tough at first. He was three years behind, struggling with English, maths—almost every subject. The gap was wide. Still, he never gave up. Night after night, he sat with his books, reading, practising, pushing forward. His focus was unshakeable.

Soon, his progress was remarkable. In just a short time, he closed much of the gap and was only a year behind. His teachers took notice—amazed by his discipline and speed of learning. The once shy, unsure boy was standing taller. Even his hand, once fused and weak, had become stronger.

We spoke often. With each visit, we saw how much he had grown. Evenings were spent listening to him talk about school, his dreams, and his wish to one day support his mother and sister.

MacKenzie carried India with her too. Her life moved ahead, but her heart never quite left. She spoke of those years with such warmth—India had shaped her just as deeply as any classroom.

Not long after we left, disturbing news broke about the orphanage.

A Telugu news channel exposed the director's horrific scheme—sending teenage girls to late-night "events" for money. Several girls bravely came forward and shared what they had endured. The police arrested the director, but the damage was already done.

Pris and I felt sick. How had we once trusted that place?

Thankfully, the authorities stepped in and relocated the children to safer shelters.

And we were grateful—Prashanth had never gone back there.

Later, after settling in Southern California, a new opportunity brought us back to India again. Several companies invited us to lead leadership and team-building programmes for their executives. What started as consulting soon turned into something deeper—an ongoing commitment to a country that had given us so much.

## An Unexpected Call

Then, in late 2010, I received an unexpected offer. HCL Technologies, one of India's leading IT services companies, wanted me to join as their Chief Learning Officer. This role brought me into collaboration with Vineet Nayar, the company's visionary CEO. Renowned for his unconventional management philosophy, Vineet had captured his ideas in his book *Employees First, Customers Second*. His radical approach emphasised empowering employees as the true catalysts of success—an idea that challenged deeply ingrained corporate hierarchies.

Intrigued, I read his book cover to cover and found myself wondering—how had he implemented such a forward-thinking strategy in a traditionally hierarchical corporate culture? On impulse, I sent him a message. I did not expect a reply.

Then, one evening, my phone rang.

"Please hold for Mr Vineet Nayar," a voice on the other end said.

A moment later, Vineet's voice came through—calm, measured, yet full of energy.

"I like your thinking," he said. "And I appreciate your message."

I was taken aback. "I have to admit, I did not expect to hear from you directly."

He laughed. "Why not?"

"Well, for one, you're the CEO of a multi-billion-dollar company. And two—" I hesitated. "Your book challenges the very fabric of corporate power structures. I had to know—how did you get buy-in? How did you convince leaders in such a hierarchical system that employees should come first?"

There was a pause.

"I did not convince them," he said. "I proved it. And it is still an ongoing effort."

He explained how he had flipped the traditional pyramid, shifting power from managers to employees by making processes transparent and holding leaders accountable to the workforce, rather than the other way around.

"You see, Ed," he said, "change does not start from the top or the bottom. It starts in the middle—where friction exists. You have to create discomfort before you create transformation."

His words struck a chord.

Several conversations later, those discussions led to something unexpected.

"I want you to come here," Vineet said one evening. "Be our Chief Learning Officer. Help me drive this forward."

I was silent for a moment. This was no small decision.

"You're asking me to relocate to India full-time?" I asked.

"Yes," he replied. "Are you in?"

I exhaled. I already knew my answer—it wasn't what he expected.

"I cannot relocate full-time," I said. "I can commit to it every other month. One month in India, one month at home in America."

There was a pause.

"Every other month?" he asked.

"Yes," I said. "That is my offer."

A few seconds passed, and then, to my surprise, he laughed.

"That's unconventional," he said. "But then again, so am I."

And just like that, we had an agreement.

## Prashanth's Return to His Village

By the time he turned sixteen, Prashanth's thoughts drifted homeward. Taller now, more assured, he felt the pull of his roots. He returned to his village—the place where his journey had begun, to the family that had once felt sending him to the orphanage was his only chance for a future. The dusty paths, the familiar clang of the temple bell, the shuffle of neighbours who now barely recognized him ... it was all the same, and yet everything had changed.

His mother and sister, who had spent years with only memories of him, now saw before them a young man transformed. There were no dramatic reunions, no flood of words—just acceptance. An understanding that life had come full circle.

We stayed in touch through phone calls and the occasional visit. As time passed, the calls grew less frequent, and life carried each of us forward in different directions.

Then, one day, a message arrived. Simple, unassuming.

"Uncle, I am now married. I have a son."

I stared at the screen for a long moment.

In that instant, his entire journey unfolded before me—from a young boy at the orphanage, his fingers fused by burns, to a man who had built a life, a family, a future of his own.

There was nothing more to say. He had found his path.

## Maintaining Our Ties with India

Our journey did not end when we left India. Our time in Noida lasted a little over a year before I faced serious health challenges that made it necessary for us to return to the United States. First, I suffered from bacterial pneumonia, which was difficult enough on its own. Then, a series of severe infections followed, leading to multiple hospital stays and surgeries. It became clear that I needed to focus on my recovery, and staying in India full-time was no longer an option.

Even after we returned, our bond with India remained strong. Almost every year, we made it a point to visit for a month or two, reconnecting with friends, colleagues, and those who had become like family.

Looking back, our time in India was never just about work. It was about learning to lead in a different culture, understanding change at its core, and building relationships that would last a lifetime. Even though our stay in Noida was shorter than expected, the impact of that chapter has stayed with me ever since.

Over the years, we remained in touch with Prashanth, and others. Some relationships only grew stronger, deepening with time as we continued to share milestones, challenges, and meaningful conversations. These connections became a lasting part of our lives, reinforced by our regular visits to India.

With Devi, however, things were different. From 2009 till 2013, Devi had no way to reach us. She didn't have a mobile phone or a computer, and she had no idea how to find us again.

Later, when she finally got access to a computer and created a Facebook account, she began searching—typing in our names, one by one, trying different combinations. She searched for mine. For Pris's. She kept going until, finally, her sister recognised our faces in a photo.

They also had an old Satyam Computers visiting card of mine tucked away somewhere—with my full name. That helped them confirm it.

She never stopped trying. She just didn't have the means—until that moment.

At first, we assumed it was a natural drift. People get busy, priorities change.

But as time passed without a word, we began to wonder—what had happened?

Our messages went unanswered. Slowly, reluctantly, we had to accept the silence.

These experiences—both the relationships that deepened and those that faded—shaped our time in India and beyond.

They reminded us of a truth we had come to know well:

Some connections grow deeper with time.

Some naturally drift apart.

But each one leaves an imprint, shaping our journey in its own way.

Even silence, we learned, can be part of the story.

# Chapter 16

# Reaching Out Across Time

The small screen cast a soft glow in the darkened room, illuminating two faces—mine and Jyothi's—as we sat huddled together, knees touching, our breaths slow and measured. The air was thick with anticipation, a mix of excitement and hesitation that neither of us spoke aloud. Outside, the whirr of a ceiling fan mixed with the sounds of a distant auto horn— Hyderabad at night, unchanged.

For years, MacKenzie, Ed Uncle, and Pris Aunty had been a distant yet ever-present force in my life—a thread woven so deeply into my past that, even as life pulled us apart, their impact had never truly faded.

I had always wondered—where were they now?

What were they doing?

Did they still think of me?

Did they ever wonder where I had ended up?

## Finding Them

And then, one evening, Facebook opened a door to the past.

It started as a simple search.

Jyothi and I sat cross-legged on the floor, her phone cradled between us. The screen reflected the faintest trace of uncertainty in our eyes as we typed.

"Ed Cohen"

The letters stared back at us, weightless yet heavy with the years in between.

A list of names appeared. Some were unfamiliar. Some held no resemblance.

Then—

There.

His face.

Older than I remembered, the lines on his face a little deeper—and unmistakably him.

For a moment, neither of us spoke. It felt surreal, as if we had conjured him out of memory, as if time had folded in on itself, bridging the years between then and now.

"Should we send him a request?" Jyothi whispered, nudging me gently.

I swallowed hard. Would he remember me?

A part of me was afraid.

What if we were just a small, forgotten part of his story? What if my name, my face, was nothing more than a faint blur in the background of a much larger life?

I stared at his profile, reading through his recent posts, looking at pictures of the life he had built since those days. Still doing what he always did—teaching, inspiring, changing lives.

And here I was, too—

a Network and Security Engineer for a data centre.

A title had once only dared to whisper, a future I had only seen in dreams. And yet, here it was. Real. Mine. Now I walked through server rooms and monitored systems—spaces that once felt unreachable.

And part of me knew—I owed some of it to him.

Not because he had handed me anything, but because of the moments when he had believed in me, when he had seen me for more than just a girl from a struggling family.

I tapped my finger against the screen, hovering over the "Send Friend Request" button.

My heart pounded.

"What if he doesn't remember?" I murmured.

Jyothi smiled knowingly, nudging me again. "And what if he does?"

I exhaled slowly. She was right.

Before I could think too much—before doubt could steal the moment—I clicked.

Sent.

We stared at the screen, waiting. Watching.

Nothing.

The notification bar remained silent. The request sat untouched.

A minute passed.

Then another.

And then an hour.

I forced myself to put the phone down.

"He's busy. He gets a lot of requests. He probably won't even see it."

Days passed.

I checked my notifications more than I cared to admit. Still nothing.

By the third day, I told myself to let it go. Maybe life had simply moved on. Maybe we were never meant to reconnect.

And then—

## A Notification

A single, simple sentence that sent my heart racing.

"Ed Cohen accepted your friend request."

A part of my past, long quiet, had suddenly reappeared.

I stared at the screen, rereading the words as if they might disappear.

He had seen my name. He remembered me.

Now, another hesitation took hold.

I had spent so long imagining this moment, wondering if I would ever get the chance to tell him what he had meant to me.

Now that it was here, my fingers trembled over the keyboard.

What if he had only accepted out of courtesy?

What if I had built this moment up in my mind for years, only to find that time had made it smaller, insignificant?

I typed a message.

Then deleted it.

I typed another.

Then erased that one, too.

I closed my laptop.

"I'll message him tomorrow."

Tomorrow came, and I still didn't.

What if he didn't feel the same way I did?

On the fourth day, I knew I couldn't wait any longer.

I took a deep breath and finally typed the words I had been holding onto for years:

"Ed Uncle, I hope you remember me."

I hit send before I could second-guess myself.

When I woke up the next morning and checked my phone, I saw his response. He had responded within minutes—but I had fallen asleep, too anxious to wait.

"Devi, I could never forget you. How are you!"

I exhaled, a laugh escaping before I even realised it.

I smiled without meaning to. I could almost hear his voice, the same warmth, the same certainty.

The same unwavering belief in me that had been there all those years ago.

## The Words I Had Waited to Say

We set up a video call and the moment his face appeared on my screen, the years fell away in a heartbeat.

He looked different—greyer, maybe—but still the same Ed Uncle.

The man who had never made me feel like I was asking for too much simply by wanting more.

"I didn't waste it," I told him, my voice steady now.

He smiled, the familiar warmth lighting up his face. "I knew you wouldn't."

I took a deep breath. "I have graduated. And, I wanted to tell you in person …Uncle."

His eyes softened. "You earned this, Devi. I'm so happy for you."

I shook my head. "Maybe. But you saw something in me I hadn't yet seen in myself."

Before I could say more, he was already calling out, his voice warm. "Pris, come see! It's Devi. She's all grown up now—and she graduated!" His voice swelled with pride, as if he had been waiting for this moment all along.

Aunty's face appeared on the screen, looking just the same—calm, steady, the warmth in her eyes unchanged.

"Devi!" Pris Aunty's voice carried across the screen, gentle yet full of affection. "Look at you! You have done so well." Somewhere in the background, I heard MacKenzie's laugh. I smiled instinctively—some bonds don't fade.

I nodded, a small smile forming, feeling the comfort of her words. "Aunty … I wanted to tell you myself. I graduated."

She clasped her hands together, her face lighting up. "That's wonderful, Devi. We knew you would do it. You worked so hard."

I swallowed, emotion pressing against my chest. "It was only possible because of all of you. Because you knew I could do it"

Aunty shook her head. "No, Devi. You did the hard work. We only supported you."

And they had.

Ed Uncle, Pris Aunty, MacKenzie—they had stood by me when I had nothing but dreams.

Pris Aunty had opened her heart and home, treating me as if I had always belonged.

MacKenzie had been the first to see me as more than the girl from next door—she had seen a friend.

And Ed Uncle … he had simply believed.

Even before I had believed in myself.

Not out of obligation, not as charity, but because he saw something in me worth believing in.

I swallowed hard, my throat tightening. So many words, so many emotions, yet nothing felt big enough to say what I truly meant.

"What you gave me ... I still carry it with me every day." I said.

He shook his head before I could go on. His expression was steady, warm, the way it had always been.

"You already have," he said simply.

Silence stayed between us—not uncomfortable, but filled with everything that didn't need to be spoken.

For so many years, I was carrying the weight of proving myself—that I was enough. That I was worthy. That I had truly done something in life—not only for me, but for Amma, for Jyothi, and for those who believed in me even when I had doubted myself.

## After Graduation

After finishing my graduation, Ed Uncle came to India for a visit and took me out for lunch. It was just the two of us, along with one senior executive from a big tech company. Because of that interaction, I got an internship. At the same time, I was also giving tuition (tutoring) to school children. I used to earn three thousand rupees from the internship and another nine thousand from tutoring. I was doing whatever I could—learning, earning, standing on my own feet.

Everything did not go smoothly. My first job after college, that he helped me to get, I left in just four days. I wasn't understanding the testing tools properly, and I didn't feel ready. I was feeling confused—like maybe I wasn't cut out for this kind of role. So I sent a message to Ed Uncle, explaining what happened.

He immediately replied and asked me, "Why did you leave?"

I told him everything—how I felt lost, how nothing made sense, how I thought maybe this job wasn't for me.

He did not scold me. He did not raise his voice. But what he said next stayed with me forever:

"I understand, Devi. But I cannot help you now. You have to stand on your own feet. This part of the journey—you must walk by yourself."

It hurt to hear those words, especially from someone who had always been there. Deep inside, I understood what he meant. That was the moment something changed inside me.

That day, I told myself—enough is enough. From now on, whether I fall or rise, it will be by my own efforts.

And from that day onwards, I did exactly that. I stood on my own. I learned to trust myself. And I started moving forward again.

I started searching seriously and was soon selected for a job at Cognizant. I worked there for a few years, slowly building experience, confidence, and some peace of mind also. When I got the offer letter, the first person I messaged was Ed Uncle. Then, I spent a year in Pune working for Infosys. I was away from my family and missed them.

I did the same when I got the job at Microsoft. I just wanted to share the news with him. Because these achievements—they were written into our destiny, one step at a time, one open door after another.

These days, I sit beside my sister Jyothi's children—my niece Karthika and nephew Gurusai—as they prepare for their tenth class board exams. I guide them through their lessons, just like I once sat on the driveway, balancing books on my knees under a flickering streetlight, dreaming of a different life.

I'm not trying to repay a debt—because what was given to me came from the heart, and you can't repay love like that. Instead, I choose to pay it forward. That's how true change happens—not by settling accounts, but by carrying kindness forward.

Someone believed in me when I had nothing—not even a proper place to study. Now, it's my turn to be that person for them. I remind them every day that their future matters, that they are capable, and that their dreams are worth chasing.

This is not about duty—it's about continuing the chain of belief. That is how we build a better world.

Every achievement, every late night hunched over textbooks, every battle with self-doubt—it was all, in some way, an attempt to honour the faith they placed in me, back when I had nothing but hope.

I wasn't just trying to prove myself to the world.

I wasn't proving it to the world. I was proving it to the little girl who dared to dream beneath a streetlamp.

And at last, I think she believes me.

# Chapter 17

# Removing My Mask

The last time we had been in India was 2017. Now, it was January 2020, and we were on our way back.

This time, I was returning without the mask to hide behind.

For decades, I had worn it well—the polished executive, the mentor, the leader who always had the right words. I had built a career by being the person who could walk into any room and command attention, who could offer solutions, inspire teams, and develop leaders. Beneath it all was a man who had carried scars—some visible, most hidden beneath layers of carefully constructed composure.

India was the place where that mask had first started to crack.

Not in a dramatic, world-shifting moment. Not through a thunderous awakening. It was in the quiet, often unnoticed moments that gently unraveled the armor I had spent a lifetime crafting.

It had been in the way people welcomed us into their homes with open arms, pressing warm food into our hands, saying "please eat" with a sincerity that left no room for formality. It had been in the humility of senior leaders who sat on the floor during team meals, their titles forgotten, their egos tucked away. It had been in the resilience of those who had so little—like Prashanth from the village—who carried themselves with a dignity that came not from wealth, but from spirit.

And it had been in Devi's eyes. Her fire. Her refusal to give up—even when every force around her whispered that she should.

Here, I didn't need to pretend.

India held up a mirror to me—not to the polished professional, but to the man behind the mask. The man with stories. The man with silence. The man who was still learning to be whole.

It showed me that leadership isn't about always knowing. It's about being present.

Being real.

Being human.

And now, I was coming back—not as the consultant with credentials, not as the speaker with slides—as someone willing to show up fully, just as I am.

Pris and I had built our life in America. Our daughter, our careers, our home. Yet India had never let go of us.

It was the land that had welcomed us when we needed it most.

Where we had built something larger than a job. We had built belongings.

We weren't coming back as guests.

We were coming back to the place that had shaped us, more than we ever shaped it.

Of all the things I looked forward to, one moment stood above the rest—seeing Devi again.

I had followed her journey online—each milestone, each photo, each triumph.

The little girl who once hovered in our dining room, unsure if she was allowed to take up space, had become a Network and Security Engineer.

She had found her voice, her path. She had claimed her future.

As we packed our bags, I caught Pris smiling at me.

"You've been talking about Devi all week," she said, a twinkle in her eye.

I grinned. "She's really done it, Pris. She didn't just escape a difficult story—she rewrote it."

For all my years in boardrooms and leadership retreats, this—this one life transformed—was what truly mattered.

Because leadership isn't about titles.

It's not about the frameworks we design or the accolades we collect.

It's about the lives we touch.

The belief we offer when someone else is barely holding on.

Devi had taken the belief we had in her and built something extraordinary. Not just for herself—but for every girl who had been told "no."

Now, I needed to see it for myself.

## Reconnecting With the Past

When we landed, India wrapped around us like an old shawl—familiar, textured with memory, and gently fragrant.

The rush of warm air as we stepped off the plane. The chaos of the taxi queue. The hum of rickshaws, street vendors, and temple bells in the distance. The distinct scent of masala and monsoon dust. It was all there. And yet … everything had changed.

We had returned many times over the years, but this visit felt different.

More tender. More personal.

I wasn't just returning to India. I was returning to the version of myself that had first found clarity here.

The first few days were spent shaking off jet lag, falling back into rhythm. The sound of the pressure cooker at dawn. Chai with ginger and tulsi leaves. Familiar faces, familiar roads. And beneath it all—anticipation.

Three nights later, we gathered for the reunion.

The Satyam School of Leadership family came together— faces we had known since they were fresh out of college, now seasoned professionals, entrepreneurs, parents. The energy in the room was electric. Not the kind that demands attention, but the kind that settles into your bones and makes you feel safe.

Then came Devi.

She walked in with a confidence I hadn't yet seen in her before. It wasn't loud or performative. It was anchored. Rooted. Her posture spoke of someone who knew her worth—not because the world handed it to her, but because she had claimed it.

She met my eyes and smiled. The little girl was gone. The same girl who once hesitated to speak beyond a whisper now stood tall—having faced board exams, job interviews, and life itself—and came through with grace. The woman in her place had built something real.

From across the room, Nayana approached with joy, her sari pleats perfectly in place, a soft glow in her eyes. She reached out and hugged Devi tightly, then stepped back and said with emotion: *"Nuvvu naa hrudayam gelichavamma."* (You've won my heart, dear.)

Devi's smile deepened, her shoulders lifting slightly—as if those words had set something free inside her.

And then there was Prashanth.

Twenty now, taller, more grounded …

The last time I saw him, he was still unsure of his place in the world. Now, he moved through the room with ease—chatting, laughing, fully himself.

He embraced me with warmth and presence. We caught up. We laughed. And in his voice, I could hear the echoes of a thousand moments I hadn't known would matter this much.

That night, the circle grew wide.

More than a hundred of us came together—Sunita, Naveen, Kishore, Nandini, Pragnya, Arvind, and so many others. Hari hosted us—once a young dreamer, now a global entrepreneur.

And what made it even more special was who joined us—young adults who had once been children in the orphanage we visited all those years ago. Some married. Some have graduated from university. All working. All thriving.

It wasn't just a reunion. It was a moment of reckoning. A reminder of what belief, encouragement, and shared purpose could truly do.

## A Verse, A Mirror

Later that night, as the room quieted and the candles flickered low, I stepped outside. The Hyderabad night was still and warm, perfumed with jasmine. A temple bell rang in the distance. Somewhere, a flute played faintly.

And in that stillness, something rose within me. A verse I had once studied—one that had stayed with me all these years—surfaced not as a line of scripture, but as truth:

"Uddhared ātmanātmānam. nātmānam avasādayet,
Ātmaiva hyātmano bandhur ātmaiva ripur ātmanah."
—*Bhagavad Gita* 6.5

Which means:
Let a person lift themselves by their own self;
let them not degrade themselves.
For the self alone is the friend of the self,
and the self alone is the enemy of the self.
That night, those words weren't just ancient wisdom.
They were a mirror. A reflection of everything I had just witnessed.

Devi had lifted herself—again and again—when no one else would. Just like Arjuna in the *Bhagavad Gita*—paralysed by doubt before the battle—Devi had once stood uncertain, afraid to take the next step. And just like in the *Gita*, someone stood beside her and whispered, "You can."

Prashanth had chosen self-worth over self-doubt. Like so many before him, he had been told—silently and aloud—that he wasn't meant to rise. But he had. Not because someone pulled him forward, but because someone had reminded him he could take the step himself.

The young adults from the orphanage had risen not because someone carried them, but because someone once said, I see you.

That verse stayed with me—not as scripture, but as a reminder of what I had seen with my own eyes.

It is not a call to independence in the Western sense.

It is a call to inner strength, to integrity, to remembering that we hold both the poison and the antidote within us.

I have been both a friend and the enemy of myself.

I have silenced my truth to fit in.

I have questioned my value more times than I care to admit.

But I have also learned—slowly, stubbornly, sacredly—that I can choose.

I can lift myself.

And in doing so, I can lift others.

That night, I knew: every life that had flourished, every journey that had taken root, wasn't just about systems or strategies. It was about moments. Conversations. Simple belief.

It was about lifting.

As I looked around—at the glow of the lights, at Devi laughing with her peers, Prashanth speaking with confidence, at children who had become men and women—I understood something I had spent decades chasing.

The greatest measure of a life is not what we build.

It's who we lift.

The people.

The belief.

The ripple effect of simply saying, "You belong."

Somewhere along the way, India had healed me.

And standing there, in the land that had cracked me open, I knew: I had come back—not just to India. To myself.

This land did not just welcome me. It reminded me who I truly was.

# Part 4
# Leading with Vulnerability

"People respond to leadership in a very personal way. They want to know that their leader cares about them."

—Narayana Murthy, Founder of Infosys

# Chapter 18

# Authentic Leadership Transforms Lives

For years, leadership was rooted in the belief that leaders must be unshakeable—confident, decisive, and immune to challenges. Vulnerability was seen as a weakness, something to be hidden behind a facade of strength. Leaders were expected to project authority, believing their role was to display control and competence. Corporate environments reinforced this myth. Showing emotion or admitting uncertainty was seen as a risk, something that could weaken influence and respect.

This mindset shaped me. I grew up with it. I saw it in leadership models around me. In my early career, I even wore the mask of invulnerability. I thought appearing perfect would make me a stronger leader. The belief was clear—a leader must have all the answers, always be in control, and never show cracks in their armour. It was a corporate expectation. It was also a personal one.

I worked hard to maintain this image of infallibility. I suppressed doubts and fears, convinced that proving my strength constantly was the only way to lead. The pressure was immense. Leadership became about maintaining an image rather than connecting with people. I felt isolated, carrying everything alone, pretending to have it all figured out. At the time, it seemed necessary. I thought it was the only way to earn respect.

But over time, my perspective evolved.

Devi changed that. She was a young girl in India, facing hardships beyond imagination. Yet, she refused to let them define her. Her strength and resilience stood out. Even in pain, she remained open and compassionate. She embraced her vulnerability instead of hiding it. That became her strength.

She taught me a lesson that changed everything. Vulnerability is not weakness. It is courage. True leadership is not about having all the answers. It is about being real, being open, and leading with heart.

It was through my relationship with Devi that I began questioning the leadership models I had followed for years. I realised that vulnerability is not a liability but a powerful tool for connection and growth. Watching Devi's resilience, I saw a truth I had long ignored. The best leaders are not those who appear invulnerable. They are the ones who embrace their humanity.

Research confirms this. A 2024 study by Gallup found that teams led by vulnerable leaders experienced a 25% increase in engagement (Gallup, 2024). Employees felt more connected to their leaders, more willing to share ideas, and more confident in taking risks. Google's Project Aristotle, a multi-year study on team effectiveness, reaffirmed that psychological safety—a culture where employees feel comfortable expressing themselves without fear—was the most critical factor in building high-performing teams (Duhigg, 2016). Leadership that fosters openness and emotional intelligence drives success in ways that rigid, hierarchical models never can.

Then, there was Prashanth. A boy who had endured unthinkable hardship, he had every reason to retreat into silence, to hide his pain. But instead, he chose openness. He let me see his scars—both physical and emotional. In turn, he allowed me to acknowledge my own. Through him, I learned that true connection is built not on perfection but on shared experiences of struggle, resilience, and healing.

At first, I resisted the idea that leadership could be anything other than a display of strength. I thought that appearing vulnerable would make me seem weak or incapable. But experience changed me. Vulnerability fosters trust. It deepens relationships. It creates space for creativity and collaboration. McKinsey & Company's 2024 research found that companies where leaders practiced vulnerability saw higher levels of innovation and problem-solving (McKinsey & Company, 2024). Employees were more willing to take risks because they knew their leaders valued honesty and growth over perfection.

As I embraced vulnerability, I realised something profound. I wasn't just leading better—I was leading in a way that felt true to who I am. Leadership based on control and perfection does not create real transformation. Leadership based on human connection, empathy, and growth does.

This shift wasn't easy. At first, it was uncomfortable. But it became one of the most rewarding lessons of my career. The most effective leaders are those who create environments where people feel safe to be themselves. Where employees feel seen, heard, and valued. Where strength is not measured by invulnerability, but by the courage to show up authentically.

True strength is not about appearing invincible. True strength is the courage to be real. To admit flaws. To create spaces where vulnerability is welcome. That is what makes a leader truly powerful.

## Vulnerability is Not a Weakness; It's a Powerful Tool

When leaders embrace vulnerability, they lead with authenticity. They inspire trust. They create environments where people feel valued and understood. Research proves this. Leaders who practice vulnerability build more engaged, creative, and resilient teams. The impact goes beyond them. It spreads across the organisation.

Employees feel safer. They express themselves freely. They contribute more. They innovate. They stay loyal. Studies show that vulnerability drives positive organisational change. It helps leaders navigate challenges. It strengthens teams.

Gallup (2024) found that teams with vulnerable leaders saw a 25% rise in engagement. Vulnerability does not just build trust. It deepens connections. It makes work more meaningful.

Google's Project Aristotle (2024) reinforced this. Their research identified psychological safety—the freedom to take risks and speak openly—as the most critical factor for high-performing teams. McKinsey & Company (2024) confirmed it. Their study showed that vulnerable leadership enhances performance. It encourages employees to share ideas. It sparks creativity. It leads to better solutions.

Vulnerability is not a weakness. It is a strength. It transforms leaders. It transforms teams. It transforms organisations.

When leaders demonstrate vulnerability, they create a culture of openness within their teams. This openness encourages team members to share their ideas, concerns, and feedback without fear of judgment. In such an environment, individuals feel valued and understood, leading to better collaboration and more effective problem-solving.

When leaders acknowledge their own challenges or uncertainties, they appear more human. This makes it easier for others to relate to them and engage authentically. Such mutual understanding fosters a workplace where diverse perspectives are welcomed, and collective intelligence flourishes (LeaderFactor, 2023).

A leader's willingness to be vulnerable plays a crucial role in fostering psychological safety within a team. Psychological safety is built on interpersonal trust and mutual respect, allowing individuals to take risks and express themselves without fear of negative consequences.

This foundation is essential for innovation. When people feel safe, they are more likely to share ideas, challenge assumptions, and step into the unknown. Research suggests that such environments lead to higher levels of creativity and engagement, as individuals are not restricted by the fear of failure or criticism (Grant Thornton, 2020).

Trust is the foundation of every successful team, and vulnerability is how we build it. When leaders share openly—about mistakes, doubts, even fears—it signals to others that they can do the same. That honesty is not punished, but welcomed. It creates a culture where people aren't hiding behind masks, where learning and risk-taking become part of the everyday rhythm of work.

Creating psychological safety wasn't limited to boardrooms or leadership teams—it started in living rooms, classrooms, and sometimes, on the ground outside an orphanage. Whether with my corporate teams or the children we mentored, the principle was the same: people thrive when they feel seen, heard, and safe.

With our teams, we built this trust through honest conversations, active listening, and shared vulnerability. And with the children, it was about showing up consistently, treating them with dignity, and believing in their potential long before the world did.

I still remember sitting with a group of children who had lived through unimaginable loss. Many had been silenced by life's circumstances. And yet, when they saw that we weren't there to judge or fix—but simply to care—they slowly began to open up. Over time, they began to dream again, speak again, and trust again. The same pattern repeated itself with teams in crisis: once safety found its footing, confidence and creativity followed.

Leaders who create this space—whether in an office, a school, or a community—lay the foundation for true innovation. They make it possible for others to grow, to challenge themselves, and to rise.

Leaders who embrace vulnerability help create workplaces where people feel valued and understood. When employees know that their voices are heard and that their contributions matter, they naturally become more engaged.

An engaged employee is more committed to their role, more productive in their efforts, and more likely to stay with the organisation. In one of the teams I led, we experienced less than 2 per cent voluntary turnover—not for a quarter or a year, but consistently, year after year. This wasn't due to extravagant perks or fancy titles. It happened because people felt a deep sense of belonging. They stayed because they were part of something meaningful, surrounded by a culture of mutual respect, purpose, and care.

This kind of culture doesn't come by chance. It is built—slowly, intentionally—when leaders lead from the heart. When employees see their leaders as approachable and empathetic, it builds trust, enhances job satisfaction, and makes the workplace feel like a community.

Embracing vulnerability also means being willing to admit mistakes and learn from them. In many organisations, errors are hidden or denied. But in teams where vulnerability is embraced, mistakes become opportunities for learning. It encourages people to take responsibility, to grow, and to support one another.

When blame is replaced with curiosity, teams become more adaptable. When failure is seen as part of the journey, people become more willing to experiment and try new ideas. That's when true innovation begins to flourish.

## Transforming Through Connection and Resilience

Integrating vulnerability into leadership is not a weakness. It is a strategic approach to building stronger, more innovative, and engaged teams. By fostering environments where authenticity, trust, and psychological safety are prioritised, leaders can drive meaningful change and achieve lasting success.

The journey towards embracing vulnerability may be challenging, but the rewards—both personal and organisational—are profound. As leaders model vulnerability, they create cultures that celebrate openness, creativity, and continuous growth, ultimately leading to more resilient and successful organisations.

The idea of vulnerability is closely linked to resilience in leadership. Resilience refers to a leader's ability to navigate challenges while maintaining performance, fostering adaptability, and encouraging perseverance within teams.

Resilient leaders create a positive impact by helping their teams thrive despite adversity. Research from the Centre for Creative Leadership (2020) highlights that resilient leaders practise compassionate leadership and authentic communication. These qualities contribute to a healthier work environment and greater team success.

This resilience not only benefits leaders personally but also drives organisational growth, ensuring that teams remain motivated and high-performing even during uncertain times.

## When "Yes" Is Not Yes

At the start of my journey in India, nothing frustrated me more than this one word: yes.

In the United States, "yes" is a commitment. It means something is happening. You can mark it on your calendar and move on. In India, I quickly learned that "yes" could mean many things—and not all of them meant "yes."

People would say, "I'll try my level best," or "Let me see what I can do," or "It might be possible." At first, I took these phrases at face value. But deadlines came and went. Deliverables stalled. And when I followed up, I was met with silence, hesitation, or vague updates.

I was confused—and, honestly, I was irritated. I began to wonder if people were being evasive or avoiding accountability. Why wasn't anyone telling me the truth?

It took time, reflection, and a bit of humility to understand that the problem wasn't honesty—it was cultural wiring. In Indian culture, saying "no" outright—especially to someone in a leadership role—is considered disrespectful. People avoid causing loss of face, even unintentionally. So rather than decline directly, they offer respectful responses that maintain harmony but don't always clarify the outcome.

Pris, as always, cut to the heart of it. One evening, after I came home from yet another ambiguous meeting, she looked at me and said:

"They're not saying yes to the task. They're saying yes to the relationship."

That's when it clicked.

The tension I felt wasn't about resistance. It was about respect. I had to shift my own mindset—from expecting directness to learning to listen between the lines.

We began co-creating what I came to call a micro-culture—a working agreement where both sides understood and adapted to one another. Instead of asking closed questions like, "Are we on track for Friday?" I learned to ask, "What remains to be done before Friday?" or "What obstacles might delay this?" We created clear communication protocols, shared accountability, and check-ins that didn't rely on vague affirmations.

Over time, the frustration gave way to understanding. The conflict became a collaboration.

This experience shaped not just my leadership—it reshaped me.

In India, I learned that progress doesn't always follow a straight line, that silence isn't indifference, and that leadership requires more than clarity—it requires cultural humility.

That's the essence of authentic leadership. You don't just lead across cultures. You grow through them.

## Understanding Reciprocal Mentorship

One of the most profound leadership shifts I have experienced is the understanding and application of reciprocal mentorship, also known as two-way mentoring. This is a dynamic relationship where both the mentor and mentee engage in mutual learning and growth. It emphasises equality and shared development, ensuring that both participants benefit from the exchange.

What makes this kind of mentorship so impactful is that it disrupts the traditional hierarchy. Rather than positioning the mentor as the superior, all-knowing figure, two-way mentoring reframes the relationship as a partnership, where both individuals contribute their unique knowledge and lived experiences. I have seen first-hand how this mutual exchange leads to growth—not just for the mentee, but also for the mentor. This is the true power of reciprocal mentorship.

In my own journey—particularly while mentoring individuals in both personal and professional contexts—I have experienced immense growth by being open to learning from those I was guiding. There were times when I believed I was imparting wisdom. Yet, as the conversations unfolded, I often realised that I was learning just as much—if not more—from those I was supposed to be helping.

I recall one moment when I began mentoring a young professional. She was early in her career but had an extraordinary ability to question established practices and challenge assumptions in ways I had never considered. While I thought I was mentoring her, she was mentoring me just as much—encouraging me to view problems from a fresh perspective. This reciprocal dynamic helped me evolve into a more reflective and adaptable leader.

The beauty of reciprocal mentorship lies in its ability to foster inclusivity and belonging in the workplace. It creates an environment where individuals feel safe to be their authentic selves, enabling the exchange of ideas and experiences that might otherwise be suppressed. Studies, such as one published by the National Institutes of Health (2022), support this idea. Research shows that participants in reciprocal mentoring programmes report increased leadership awareness, enhanced coping mechanisms, and greater confidence as leaders—highlighting the mutual benefits of these relationships. In essence, both parties learn, adapt, and grow in ways that would not be possible in a traditional, one-sided mentorship framework.

As I reflect on my leadership journey, one truth stands out above all: vulnerability is not just a leadership tool—it is a leadership revolution. The leaders I admire most—those who inspire loyalty, creativity, and innovation—are the ones who embrace their humanity. They show their authentic selves to their teams. Through vulnerability, they create environments where trust flourishes, ideas are shared freely, and individuals take risks knowing that mistakes are not failures but opportunities for growth.

This shift in my perspective—from believing leadership is about invulnerability to understanding that true strength comes from vulnerability—has reshaped both my leadership and my life. It is a lesson I continue to practise every day, in the workplace and in my personal life. The more I allow myself to be vulnerable, the more I realise how deeply connected we all are in our shared human experience. Vulnerability opens doors to connection, trust, and collaboration, creating a ripple effect that can transform teams and entire organisations.

## The Future of Leadership: Powered by Vulnerability

Looking ahead, I envision a future where vulnerability is accepted and embraced as the foundation of leadership. A future where leaders recognise that true strength does not lie in the illusion of invincibility. It lies in the courage to be authentic—to admit what they do not know, to seek input from others, and to foster environments where every voice is valued.

As this shift takes hold, our workplaces will transform. They will not only become more productive but also more compassionate, resilient, and deeply human. In these spaces, leadership will no longer be defined by authority alone but by the ability to connect, uplift, and inspire. It will not be about having all the answers. It will be about creating a culture where people feel safe enough to explore possibilities together.

I am committed to shaping this future—one where vulnerability is no longer mistaken for weakness. Instead, it will be recognised as the driving force of innovation, trust, and collective success. Because when leaders lead with openness, they do not just elevate themselves—they create a movement. A movement where people feel seen, heard, and empowered to bring their best selves forward.

This is the leadership revolution we need. And it begins with us.

This truth is simple yet profound. Every act of kindness, every moment of belief, creates ripples in ways we may not always see. When we choose to help someone—not just with resources, but with encouragement, support, and belief—we are not just changing their moment. We are changing their trajectory.

And that is only the beginning.

The real magic lies in what follows—the ripple effect.

When you uplift someone, when you believe in them, you ignite something that does not stop with them. It keeps going. They carry that kindness, that encouragement, that belief forward. They pass it on to someone else. And in turn, that person does the same.

# Chapter 19

# If I Could Speak to That Girl Again

If I could speak to that girl again—the one with dust on her feet and too many thoughts in her head—I wouldn't give her any advice.

I wouldn't tell her to be brave or patient or hopeful. She had already learned to pretend all those things.

I would just sit beside her. Not ask questions. Not offer solutions. Just stay.

Because sometimes, the hardest thing to believe is that someone might stay—without expecting anything in return.

That girl didn't think she had a voice.

She assumed her job was to take up as little space as possible. To stay quiet. To blend in. To never ask for too much.

Even with Amma—my Amma, who loved me with a fierce kind of love that didn't always have softness—there were so many things I never said.

She was always working, always worrying, stretching what little we had to cover what we didn't.

She never cried in front of us. Never complained. She just kept going.

And somewhere in my small, scared heart, I thought:

If I cry, it will make her tired.

If I ask, it will make her sad.

So I stayed quiet.

But Amma never told me to be less.

She just didn't have the space to show me how to be more.

And even so, she gave me the one thing that changed everything—she let me study, she let me dream.

Even when she didn't fully understand the world I was trying to step into, she made room for me to take that step.

And then, one day, I found myself inside a house I couldn't have imagined.

The floors were clean enough to sleep on. The food came hot, even when no one had been in the kitchen.

And Jasper, their little white dog, was the first to welcome me.

He didn't care about my clothes, my accent, or where I came from.

He just wagged his tail, like we were already family.

A sock, a patch of sunlight, a dropped bit of curry—he found joy in the smallest things.

And somehow, that was the first time I truly felt accepted.

Not by someone trying to understand me, but by someone who already had.

I didn't know how to behave in that world.

There were rules I didn't understand. Words I couldn't pronounce. Doors that opened just because I stood in front of them.

But they—MacKenzie, Pris Aunty, and Ed Uncle—never made me feel like I didn't belong.

Pris Aunty had this way of sitting beside me without forcing questions.

She never treated me like a project. She treated me like a person.

And MacKenzie—she welcomed me first. Fully. Without hesitation.

Like it was the most normal thing in the world.

Even Jasper understood. He let me cry beside him once—quietly, gently—as if he knew not to bark.

And there were others too—people from their world.

They spoke fast, dressed smart, and laughed loudly.

But they didn't flinch when they saw me.

They didn't ask me to explain myself.

They saw me as I was—and didn't look away.

That was new.

And then one day, I heard myself laugh.

It startled me. The sound came from deep within—raw and unguarded.

I froze. Had I been too loud? Had I forgotten to shrink?

But no one looked up. No one told me to stop.

And in that moment, I realised—I didn't have to shrink to be safe.

I started speaking.

Not to impress. Not to convince.

But just to say what was true.

To finally speak what had waited inside me for years.

I got into university younger than most in my class.

I didn't fit in. I didn't go to cafés. I didn't know the right words.

But I finished. On time. On merit.

I started my career and built my skills.

Then came the job. Pune.

I had never been so far from home. But I went.

I lived alone. Learned the trains. Learned the silence of an empty flat.

That's where I met Vivek.

He didn't talk too much. He didn't try to fix me.

He just listened. Then, slowly, he became my friend. My partner. My husband.

That's also when I saw Amma differently—not just as my mother, but as a woman who had bent her entire life, and still stood tall.

Today, I carry another life within me.

I don't know yet if it's a boy or a girl. But I already speak to this child.

I tell them:

You are wanted.

Your voice matters.

You don't have to earn your worth.

I tell them about Amma.

How she showed me strength without showing tears.

I tell them about the girl I used to be—who once feared her own laughter. Who mistook silence for safety.

And how, in a house filled with strangers who became family, next to a jasmine plant in full bloom, I began to find my voice.

I don't know what kind of world my child will grow up in.

But I know this much: they will carry my story. Amma's story. Our story.

And maybe, one day, they will speak it aloud.

And when they do, I hope they know—their voice was never meant to be small.

Amma used to tell me, almost like a lullaby:

"*Nee paadamettu prathi chotalo, chinna deepam veliginchagalavu.*"

Every place your foot touches, you can light a small lamp.

I never understood it then.

But now I do.

Even the softest step can spark something lasting.

And I hope my child, and their child, carry that flame forward.

I am Devi.

# Epilogue: Carry it Forward

Devi continues her journey with Microsoft—balancing career, home, and a deepening sense of purpose. She is no longer the girl who studied under a flickering streetlamp. She stepped forward when others stepped back. The first in her family to graduate, she has become a resilient leader in her own right—and now, married and a new mother, determined to pass on strength, not struggle.

As we finished this book in the mornings for me in America and then evenings for her in India, Devi sat beside her sister Jyothi's children—her niece Karthika and nephew Gurusai—as they prepared for their 10th class board exams. She guided them through their lessons, just as she once balanced books on her knees in a narrow driveway, reading under the dim streetlight, dreaming of a different life.

She never saw this as repaying a debt. What was given to her came straight from the heart—and love like that, it cannot be repaid. Instead, she chooses to carry it forward. That is how real change—not by settling accounts, but by continuing the cycle of kindness.

Someone believed in her when she had nothing—not even a proper place to sit and study. Today, she becomes that someone for them. Every day, she reminds the children that their future matters, that they are capable, and that their dreams are worth chasing.

For Devi, it is not about duty. It is about continuing a chain of belief. That is how a better world is built—little by little, heart by heart.

Every small achievement, every late night with open textbooks, every battle with self-doubt—it was all, in its own way, an offering to honour the faith placed in her when she had nothing but hope.

Her Amma, who worked as a maid just to serve food on the table, now lives with dignity and independence in the home her daughter provides. No longer cleaning others' houses—she is a cook by choice, working for two families, standing proud in a life she helped build with her own hands. The same woman who once slept in a single-room portion now opens her own front door—her steps steady, her back straight.

And Jyothi, who set aside her own dreams so Devi could follow hers, now watches her children reach the very grade that Devi once topped. What she gave up is not forgotten. Her sacrifice echoes in her children's determination—their school books, exam pads, and the soft prayers of a mother who once whispered … "Adjust Devi. Amma will come back for us."

Three women. Three journeys. One story—of resilience, and rising, together.

Pris and I now live in southern California, where we continue to guide and mentor leaders from around the world. Our daughter, MacKenzie, lives in northern California and works as a holistic healer with expertise in massage therapy and herbal medicine. Her years in India played a major role in shaping her path, nurturing a lifelong commitment to wellness and natural healing practices.

Jasper, our dog, who felt equally at home either in India or America, lived a long and joyful life of nineteen years—which is quite rare for a dog.

He was full of energy, always chasing shadows, tail wagging like a motor whenever someone came near.

He never cared where people were from, how they spoke, or what they wore.

If you showed him a little love, he gave back a whole world in return.

For many—especially those unsure of their place in the world—Jasper offered something rare: loud, playful, wholehearted affection.

His spirit, like that of a happy child, continues to live in our memories and our laughter.

With decades of experience across cultures, Pris and I remain committed to supporting individuals and organisations in creating environments rooted in empathy, purpose, and authentic leadership. Our bond with India continues—not only through memories, but through relationships that have shaped our lives and remain close to our hearts.

While working on this book with Devi, I came to know something she had never shared before.

Her father passed away when she was in 10th standard. She was just fourteen.

When she told me, I paused.

Because I, too, lost my father at a similar age. The circumstances were different, yes, but her words brought back memories I had long made peace with. Through the years— through reflection, conversations, and healing—I have found a place for that part of my story. It lives inside me quietly, no longer heavy, no longer aching.

So when Devi shared her loss, it did not feel like a wound reopening. It felt like a coincidence—one of those life moments that gently reminds you how far we have travelled. From different countries, different lives, and different kinds of loss, we have both kept moving forward.

We were both young. Both learning how to carry on.

She had never spoken of it before. Not even once.

One evening, while we were talking, she finally opened up.

She said, "One day, I came home from tuition. It was around ten in the night. I was in my 10th class, and pre-final exams were going on. When I entered, I saw everyone packed and waiting for me. I could not understand—why now, why suddenly going to Nandyal? I kept saying I have exams, I can't come. Then Amma told me ... Father passed away. We had to go now. I couldn't speak. I just cried. So many days I had been wishing he would come back. A few months before—maybe five or six—he did come. But I was angry with him for not being with us all those years. So I didn't talk to him. That was the last time I saw him … before he died. He passed away due to a heart stroke."

Her voice was soft when she spoke those words. Not bitter. Not broken. Just honest.

It takes courage to share such a memory. Even more so when it has lived in silence for so long.

That night, she wasn't just telling me about her father's death—she was showing me the strength it took to move on, without even fully understanding what she was carrying.

This is the kind of strength that shapes a life quietly. Without grand speeches. Without the world even noticing.

Maybe because she didn't want it to shape how others saw her. And truly, it hasn't. Her strength lies not in forgetting, but in continuing—gently, courageously, step by step.

This is not only a story of hardship.

It is a story of transformation—built on courage, sustained by belief, and carried forward through the lives it touches.

And perhaps, it is no coincidence that her name is Devi.

In Indian tradition, Devi is the 'divine feminine'—worshipped across the country in many forms. She is Durga, the protector of righteousness, who rides the tiger with fierce determination. She is Saraswati, the embodiment of knowledge, wisdom, and learning. She is Lakshmi, the bringer of abundance, grace, and prosperity. She is also Kali, the fierce force that removes darkness and fear.

Like the goddess, this Devi holds many aspects within her—gentleness and strength, vulnerability and power. She is proof that the divine is not only found in temples, but in classrooms, in small acts of kindness, in bold decisions, and in every girl who dares to rise beyond the expectations placed upon her.

*Worlds Apart* is meant to be more than a book. It is a reminder.

A reminder that change begins with one step. That a single act of belief can create ripples across generations.

That when we open our hearts to someone from another world, we may find our own transformed.

This is not an ending—it is an offering.

Take the 26–Week Carry It Forward Challenge:

A journey of connection, courage, and change begins with a single step.

Let these A to Z lessons not just stay with you—let them move through you.

We invite you to take on the 26-Week Carry It Forward Challenge:

Each week, choose one letter. Reflect on the lesson.

Then, complete the "Carry it Forward" action—for yourself, and, where you can, for someone else.

There's no right pace. Only a willingness to begin.

Because even the smallest act, done with sincerity, can light the path for another.

This is not a checklist—it's a transformation. A deepening. A remembering. A way to live your story out loud.

**A: Authenticity creates space for healing.**

When we stop hiding behind perfection and speak our truth—even just to ourselves—we allow healing to begin. Authenticity isn't about exposing everything; it's about no longer pretending. When we choose to be honest in moments that matter, we step into wholeness.

Carry it Forward: Share one personal truth this week—with someone you trust or even in a journal. Begin with yourself.

Reflection:

**B: Belief in someone can shape their future.**

When someone believes in us—even before we believe in ourselves—it plants a seed of possibility. That belief can become the foundation for confidence, courage, and vision. The right words at the right time can change the direction of a life.

Carry it Forward: Tell one person today what you see in them—especially if they can't see it yet.

Reflection:

**C: Courage isn't loud.**

Courage isn't always about bold gestures. It's found in persistence—in studying under a streetlamp, in asking for help, in continuing to show up despite fear. Real bravery often hides in the everyday choices to keep going.

Carry it Forward: Reflect on one act of courage you've taken in the last month. Acknowledge it, and take another small step forward this week.

Reflection:

**D: Dignity comes from being seen.**

We begin to believe in our own worth when others recognise it. Dignity isn't granted by status or wealth—it is affirmed when someone listens, includes you, or acknowledges your presence. Even the smallest gesture of respect can restore a person's sense of self.

Carry it Forward: Make someone feel seen today. Use their name, listen without interrupting, or simply acknowledge their effort.

Reflection:

**E: Empathy bridges hearts.**

Empathy doesn't require shared experience—just the willingness to feel with someone. It softens judgment and deepens connection. When we open our hearts to another's emotions, we build trust, belonging, and safety. Empathy is presence with feeling.

Carry it Forward: The next time someone shares their struggle, don't try to fix it. Just feel with them. Let that be enough.

Reflection:

**F: Fear loses power when named.**

Fear thrives when it stays in the shadows. When we speak it—write it, say it, or share it—we take away its mystery and reduce its hold. Naming fear doesn't make it vanish, but it makes it manageable. Clarity gives us back our choice.

Carry it Forward: Write down a fear you've been carrying. Say it aloud, then take one clear, small step toward it.

Reflection:

**G: Gratitude amplifies growth.**

Gratitude isn't about ignoring struggle—it's about acknowledging what sustains us through it. When we honour the people, moments, and lessons that shaped us, we deepen our resilience. Gratitude keeps us grounded and reminds us that we never journey alone.

Carry it Forward: Identify one person or experience that helped shape who you are today. Express your thanks— through a message, a phone call, or reflection.

Reflection:

**H: Hope survives even the harshest beginnings.**

Hope is not naive optimism; it is defiant faith that something better is possible—even when life has taught you otherwise. It flickers even in the darkest moments, a reminder that your story isn't over yet. Hope doesn't erase pain, but it makes room for something beyond it.

Carry it Forward: Ask yourself: "What is one thing I'm still holding on for?" Write it down and revisit it when doubt tries to dim your light.

Reflection:

**I: Impact isn't always intentional.**

We don't always realise when we've changed someone's life. A kind word, a shared meal, or a small gesture of inclusion can stay with someone forever. The most meaningful impact often comes not from grand plans, but from showing up with sincerity and consistency.

Carry it Forward: Think of a time someone made a difference in your life without knowing it. Then, live today as if your actions carry that same power—because they do.

Reflection:


**J: Joy can coexist with pain.**

Pain does not cancel joy. In fact, joy often finds its way through cracks in hardship—unexpected laughter, shared meals, a moment of peace. Allowing space for joy is not betrayal of your struggle; it's an act of resistance and renewal.

Carry it Forward: Find one moment today to choose joy—without guilt. It could be music, movement, food, or a memory. Let yourself feel it, even if life feels heavy.

Reflection:


**K: Kindness is never wasted.**

Kindness lives on, often long after the moment has passed. It may not be remembered word for word, but its effect lingers in hearts. Kindness given freely—without expectation—has the power to interrupt cycles of hurt and create new paths of connection.

Carry it Forward: Do one thing today that is kind, especially when it's inconvenient or unseen. Let it be enough that it came from you.

Reflection:

**L: Leadership is presence, not position.**

Leadership is not about titles or authority—it's about showing up, listening deeply, and standing with others in their moments of uncertainty. True leaders create space for others to rise. Their power comes not from control, but from connection.

Carry it Forward: Practice leadership today by offering presence. Ask someone how they are and truly listen. Your attention might be the leadership they need most.

Reflection:


**M: Mentorship is mutual.**

True mentorship is not a one-way gift—it's a shared exchange. When we teach, we learn. When we support, we grow. The most powerful mentorship happens when both people show up with openness, humility, and the willingness to be changed by the relationship.

Carry it Forward: Think of someone younger or newer in your circle. Offer support—but also ask them what they see that you might not. Be open to learning from their perspective.

Reflection:


**N: No one rises alone.**

Strength is often built on unseen shoulders—on someone who stood by us, helped us up, or believed in our worth. Even the most courageous journeys are carried by consistent support. Connection is not a luxury—it's essential to rising.

Carry it Forward: Reach out to someone who has helped carry your story. Thank them. If you need support now, let one person in.

Reflection:

**O: Openness invites possibility.**

When we let our guard down—even a little—we create space for new relationships, ideas, and healing. Openness isn't about trusting everyone; it's about being available to what's next. The path forward often begins with simply being willing to take a step.

Carry it Forward: Say yes to something you've been hesitant about—an invitation, a new idea, or a conversation. See what unfolds when you stay open.

Reflection:


**P: Pain doesn't define your future.**

Pain shapes us, but it does not set our destination. We are more than what happened to us. When we carry pain with awareness rather than shame, we transform it into wisdom. Our past may walk beside us, but it doesn't get to lead.

Carry it Forward: Write down one painful experience that has lingered. Next to it, write something you've learned or gained because you've lived through it.

Reflection:


**Q: Questions reveal courage.**

It takes bravery to ask the hard questions—especially the ones without easy answers. Questions like "Why not me?" or "What if I tried?" challenge the status quo and open the door to possibility. Curiosity is often the first act of hope.

Carry it Forward: Ask yourself one honest, brave question today. Sit with it. Let it guide your next small step forward.

Reflection:

**R: Resilience is nurtured, not inherited.**

Resilience isn't something you're born with—it's built over time through struggle, connection, and support. It grows each time we choose to rise, not because it's easy, but because someone believed we could. It's less about bouncing back and more about carrying forward.

Carry it Forward: Identify one way you've grown stronger through adversity. Acknowledge that resilience, and share the story with someone who may need encouragement.

Reflection:

**S: Silence can be survival, but not forever.**

Sometimes we stay silent to stay safe—but silence can also become a prison. When we find the strength to speak—even a little—we begin to reclaim our voice. Sharing your truth, when the time is right, is not only healing for you—it gives others permission to do the same.

Carry it Forward: Choose one piece of your story you've never shared. Write it for yourself, or speak it aloud in a safe space. Your voice matters.

Reflection:

**T: Trust is built in small moments everyday.**

Trust isn't built in grand moments—it's built in ordinary ones. Showing up, following through, being honest—these small choices create safety over time. Trust doesn't require perfection. It requires consistency.

Carry it Forward: Identify one relationship where trust matters. Do one small thing today to reinforce that trust— show up, follow through, or speak honestly.

Reflection:

**U: Understanding builds connection.**

When we make the effort to understand someone's journey—what shaped them, what they carry—we begin to connect more deeply. Understanding comes from listening with openness, not assumptions. It creates space for others to be fully human.

Carry it Forward: Ask someone about their story today. Listen not just to respond, but to understand.

Reflection:


**V: Vulnerability transforms.**

Being vulnerable isn't about weakness—it's about truth. When we let ourselves be seen, we create space for connection, growth, and trust. Vulnerability in leadership, in friendship, in family—it invites others to show up more fully, too.

Carry it Forward: Share one thing today that feels a little uncomfortable but real. It could be an honest emotion, an apology, or simply asking for help.

Reflection:


**W: Worth is not earned; it is inherent.**

You don't have to prove your value by achieving, pleasing, or pretending. You are worthy—just as you are. Knowing your worth is not arrogance—it's the foundation of self-respect, boundaries, and healing.

Carry it Forward: Write down three reasons why you are worthy—without mentioning anything you've done for others. Read it back whenever you forget.

Reflection:

**X: X marks the spot.**

The place where transformation begins is not far away—it's right where you are. You don't need to wait for the perfect moment, the right words, or a sign from the universe. The treasure you seek—healing, clarity, connection—often lives beneath your own feet. Growth doesn't always require movement. Sometimes it begins by standing still, and choosing to look inward.

Carry It Forward:

Pause today and ask yourself: What truth, opportunity, or strength is already within me or around me? Claim that space. That's your spot.

Reflection:


**Y: You are not your past.**

Your past may have shaped you, but it does not define your future. Growth happens when we stop letting old wounds steer the present. You are allowed to change, evolve, and outgrow the person you once had to be.

Carry it Forward: Identify one belief you hold because of your past that no longer serves you. Replace it with a new belief—and speak it out loud.

Reflection:


**Z: Zoom out to understand, zoom in to care.**

When we take a step back, we begin to see the larger context—the systems, the stories, the struggles that shape people's lives. This perspective helps us judge less and understand more. But change doesn't happen from a distance. It requires us to zoom in—to get close, to listen, to stand beside someone with presence and compassion. Understanding widens the lens; care brings the focus home.

Carry It Forward: The next time you find yourself judging a situation or person, pause. Step back to see the full picture—then step in to offer empathy, support, or simply your attention.

Reflection:

# References

Agile Leadership Journey. (2021). What's the connection between psychological safety and innovation? Retrieved from https://www.agileleadershipjourney.com/blog/whats-the-connection-between-psychological-safety-and-innovation

Forbes. (2020). 12 Benefits of Embracing Vulnerability in Leadership. Retrieved from https://www.forbes.com/councils/forbescommunicationscouncil/2020/03/02/12-benefits-of-embracing-vulnerability-in-leadership

Gallup. (2024). The Power of Vulnerability in Leadership: How Vulnerable Leaders Drive Engagement and Success. Retrieved from https://hortoninternational.com

Google's Project Aristotle. (2024). Psychological Safety and High-Performing Teams: Insights from Project Aristotle. McKinsey & Company. Retrieved from https://www.mckinsey.com

Grant Thornton. (2020). Psychological Safety Underpinning Innovation. Retrieved from https://www.grantthornton.global/en/insights/articles/Inclusively-leading-through-change/psychological-safety-underpinning-innovation

Horton International. (2024). Leaders Who Show Vulnerability Are More Likely to Build Trust, Which Is the Foundation of High-Performing Teams. Retrieved from https://hortoninternational.com

LeaderFactor. (2023). Vulnerability in Leadership: How Openness Leads to Stronger Teams. Retrieved from https://www.leaderfactor.com/learn/vulnerability-in-leadership

McKinsey & Company. (2024). Vulnerable Leadership and Innovation: How Vulnerability Enhances Organizational Performance. Retrieved from https://www.mckinsey.com

National Institutes of Health. (2022). A Study on the Impact of Reciprocal Mentorship. Retrieved from https://www.nih.gov

# Final Reflection: This Is How Transformation Happens

**How far apart can two lives begin—and still come together in a story where each of us sees a piece of ourselves?**

This is not just our story. It is yours too.

We often imagine transformation as grand—driven by influence, wealth, or position. In truth, real change begins with courage. A single decision to truly see someone—especially when the world chooses to look away.

We once believed we were offering help. Each time we extended a hand, we changed too. Kindness was never one-sided. It became a shared journey that shaped both of us.

Helping someone is not about charity. It is about dignity. It is saying: You matter. You belong. You deserve a chance.

One of the most profound truths we've come to understand is this:

"One of the deepest longings of the human soul is to be seen."
—Brené Brown

When someone truly sees you—not for where you come from, but for who you can become—it plants the seed for transformation.

This is the truth at the heart of it all: When you help one person, two people change. In giving, we grow. In lifting someone else, we rise too.

We see this reflected in the life of Kalpana Chawla, who once walked the dusty roads of Karnal and rose to the stars.

Her words continue to guide those who dare to dream:
"The path from dreams to success does exist.

May you have the vision to find it,

the courage to get on to it,

and the perseverance to follow it."

—Kalpana Chawla


Paying it forward is not merely a gesture—it becomes a movement.

Think of Dr A.P.J. Abdul Kalam. Born in Rameswaram, the son of a boatman, he sold newspapers as a boy and studied beneath a streetlamp. That image—of a child bent over books under flickering light—remains etched into India's collective memory.

A symbol of possibility, of purpose, of dreaming against all odds.

He grew to become our "Missile Man" and later, one of India's most beloved leaders—our People's President. His philosophy still inspires us to take that first step:
"Dream, dream, dream.

Dreams transform into thoughts and thoughts result in action."

—Dr A.P.J. Abdul Kalam


So here is our invitation to you:

Pay it forward. Watch the ripple grow. It need not be big. Or perfect. Or even planned. It only needs to be real.

Encourage someone who feels invisible. Offer your time. Share your belief in them. Speak a word of kindness when it matters most.

Then step back. The belief you offer takes root. It grows. It travels farther than you may ever know.

Sudha Murty reminds us why education and compassion go hand in hand:

"A good education teaches you to rise above all kinds of prejudice—be it gender, caste, or social status—and to serve others with humility and compassion."

—Sudha Murty


You may not witness the full impact of your kindness.

Still, trust that it already matters.

One act can shift a life. When a life shifts, families begin to change. As families change, communities rise. As communities rise, the nation transforms.

This is how courage creates change. This is how stories evolve. This is how we build a better Bharat—together.

There is no need to wait for the perfect moment. No need to question whether your action is enough. Never underestimate the ripple you begin.

When you help one person, two people change.

And that is how we change the world—step by step, heart to heart.

—Devi Boddu & Ed Cohen

# Acknowledgements

Writing this book has been both a joy and a mirror. It is not just a story—it is a **safar** of lives intertwined, of lessons exchanged, of people who held space for me when I didn't yet know how to ask. Some are no longer with us, but their impact remains, like diya light in a long hallway.

To all those who touched this story—**dhanyavaadamulu, shukriya, and heartfelt thanks.**

To **you**, the reader. Thank you for walking with us through this story. May you find something in these pages that helps you see yourself, or someone else, more clearly—and with more compassion.

## From Devi

To my Amma, who stood like a rock behind me. You gave me permission to dream, even when the world expected you to get me married. You believed in what I could become, even when it meant pawning your gold earrings just to meet our daily needs. I did not understand your sacrifices then, but today, I hold them close with deep gratitude. You are the strongest woman I have ever known.

To my Akka, Jyothi, my sister and second mother. You gave up your own aspirations so I could follow mine. You carried my burdens as if they were your own and made sure I was never alone. I saw the pride in your eyes at every small step forward. Your love has always been my shelter.

To my Avva (grandmother), the pillar of our family. You stood with us through our hardest times and never let go. You believed in my future long before I had the courage to imagine it. Your strength uplifted all of us.

To Vivek, my husband, my companion, my anchor. You accepted me for who I am and remained beside me through every test. Your encouragement has made me stronger, your presence brings me peace, and your faith in us gives me hope for the road ahead.

To my family—my roots and my wings. To my cousins, uncles, and everyone who stood by me—your love, blessings, and encouragement have always been my strength. I am holding your pride with folded hands and a full heart. When Amma was going through tough times, you all stood with her like a rock and even supported us financially without any hesitation. For that, I will be forever thankful. Without your support, we could not have come this far.

To Amma and Achan,

What can I say? I am truly blessed to be part of this family. After marriage, I never imagined I would receive so much love and warmth. You welcomed me not as a daughter-in-law, but as your own daughter. Amma, you never once made me feel like an outsider. You never asked me to do anything—instead, you brought food to wherever I was sitting and made all my favourite dishes with so much love. Every time I am in your home, I feel like I am in my own.

Achan, you laugh and play with me like I'm still a little girl, and our time together always brings me so much joy. Growing up, I only had Amma's side of the family—my father's side was never in the picture. I always dreamed of a big family, and now, thanks to you both, I feel complete. You accepted me and my family just as we are. You even take pride in Amma. That kind of love and acceptance is rare. What more can I say? You are truly the best.

To MacKenzie, who changed the direction of my life with one small act of kindness. You saw me. You included me. You treated me like your own from day one. Still I remember those days and I wish we could go back and relive them again. Your friendship gave me a fresh beginning.

To Ed Uncle and Pris Aunty, who turned my life around completely. You believed in me even before I believed in myself. It was not just about school fees—you gave me respect, confidence, and that feeling that I belong. Never once did you treat me like I didn't belong. Always, you made me feel like family. That love, I will carry in my heart forever.

To Raji Ma'am, who taught me how to study with heart. You used to sit with me late nights, helping me understand the lessons—especially maths! When I was ready to give up, you were the one who gently encouraged me to keep going. You showed me what real learning is. Even today, I think of you and wish I can meet you just once to say one sincere thank you.

To my dear friends, who filled my journey with joy, support, and light.

You stood beside me—during silence, during struggle, and during celebration. Your presence made all the difference. I am truly thankful to each one of you.

## From Ed

Before taking any names, I wish to speak from my heart.

To India—how shall I begin?

It may sound uncommon to thank a whole nation, yet this land transformed me. The colours, the chaos, the calm—the relationship, the resilience, the kindness in tea stalls and autorickshaws, the jugaad that turns struggle into innovation. You taught me how to lead with heart, to remain grounded even in contradiction, and to feel complete in my imperfections.

India became our second home.

To Devi—this book would not exist without you. Your courage and spirit changed all our lives. You showed me that real leadership is not about titles, but about truth and vulnerability. And to your Amma, who stood like a lioness for her daughters—Shukriya, Mahalakshmi.

To Pris—my wife, my life partner, my anchor. You were never the quiet one—and thank heavens for that. Your fierce love, quick wit, and unshakable presence carried us through every season. We didn't just walk this path—we carved it, side by side. This story is as much yours as mine.

To MacKenzie, our daughter, the one who opened her heart first. You welcomed without hesitation, loved without conditions. Your instinct to protect and uplift made space for voices that might have stayed unheard. You are a pure light in my life.

To my mother, Bernice, who is no longer with us—you shaped me more than words can express. Through your hard work, your sacrifices, and your deep belief in the power of learning, you gave me the foundation to dream.

To Aunt Audre—your home was my first true shelter. Your love was loud and unwavering, your presence healing. You made me feel seen in a world that tried to make me invisible. You planted the seeds of hope in me.

To Elana, my cousin-sister—Aunt Audre's daughter—thank you for travelling to India with your beloved Howard, and embracing our life here with warmth and openness. Your presence felt like an extension of your mother's grace.

To Jay Golub, my dearest friend since 1969—Thank you for standing by me through every version of myself. Ours is not only a friendship of time, but of trust, laughter, and loyalty that never wavered.

To Joshua Craver—when I said I was leaving Booz Allen, you said, "I want to go to Indiana with you." I laughed—"It's India, not Indiana!" Yet you trusted, and came. As you once said, "Some friends are for a reason, some for a season, and some for life." Ours is for life, my brother.

To Prashanth—you walked through so much, yet never stopped learning, never stopped trying to belong. And to your Amma, for the trust you placed in us—we always held it with honour. You made us part of your son's journey.

To the doctors of Doctors Without Borders—you healed more than just Prashanth's hand. You returned to him his independence, and with it, his dreams.

To Nishi Levitt—may your memory continue to bless us. And to David Levitt, for giving Prashanth a space to grow and feel seen. And to Nayana Chekka and her family—who welcomed Prashanth as their own—thank you for your kindness and acceptance.

To John Bastien Kennedy—not only our driver but our bridge between cultures. Your steady kindness brought comfort to our everyday life.

To Satish Kumar Chegiri, Deepika Miriyala, and Kishore Goud—you are not just friends—you are like our own children. Your laughter, love, and loyalty have made our lives richer. The bond we share is for keeps.

To Sunita Lanka, our dear friend and colleague of many years—and to Natraj, your equal in every way, and your wonderful sons Anirudh and Shreyas—thank you for walking this path with us since the beginning.

And to Venkat Acharya—our friend, guide, and spiritual teacher

Thank you for your blessings and presence.

To Pragnya Seth—what began as guidance became sisterhood. You helped us understand India not just with our heads, but with our hearts. You, your Amma Sunita, and your children Shantanu and Amala welcomed us with such warmth—we always felt like family.

To Hari Ankem—whom I've had the privilege to mentor and call a friend. Your wisdom, loyalty, and open heart have been a steady presence. I treasure our bond.

To Kavitha Thonangi—the very first to join our team in India. Your belief, dedication, and energy helped us build a foundation that still stands strong.

To Arvind Krishna—Thank you for lending your voice and heart to this book. You may be younger, but you carry a timeless soul. I am so proud of the path you walk.

To the children at the orphanage—Those whose names we knew, and those we didn't—your smiles, your strength, your light live in these pages.

To the Satyam Learning World team—Thank you for believing in learning, in growth, and in the power of transformation. You made us dream bigger.

To Dr. Justin Yanuck—Your presence gave me the courage to remember and write. You helped me speak truths I had long buried. Thank you for helping me open my heart.

## To Om Books International—

Thank you for believing in this story and giving it a home.

To the entire team led by Ajay Mago and Shantanu Ray, we are so appreciative. To the designers, copyeditors, marketers, publicists—thank you for treating each word with thoughtfulness and respect.

# Carrying It Forward

**Why I'm Donating Every Rupee from *Worlds Apart* to Educate More Girls Like Devi**

Every rupee I earn from *Worlds Apart* will go to Project Nanhi Kali, helping open doors for more girls like Devi. The heart of this story lives in India, and so does mine. Managed by the K.C. Mahindra Education Trust and Naandi, Project Nanhi Kali is one of India's leading initiatives supporting girls' education.

While my share supports more girls, Devi's royalties go directly to her. She is now married, a new mother, and continues to care for her family—proof that when a girl is given a chance, she lifts everyone around her.

If *Worlds Apart* has moved you, I invite you to carry the story forward. Sponsoring a Nanhi Kali costs about ₹6,000 a year—less than $100—and can change a life. Learn more or donate at www.nanhikali.org.

This book began with MacKenzie. She saw Devi before the rest of us did, helping both of us find our voices. It started with a simple hello. *Imagine what your hello could become.*

—Ed Cohen